Mastering Azure Fundamentals: A Comprehensive Guide to Cloud Computing with Microsoft Azure

BY

Issa Ngoie

CONTENTS

DevOps. It would cover concepts like Azure App Service, Azure SQL Database, and Azure DevOps, and provide guidance on how to architect, deploy, and manage these solutions in Azure.

Exam AZ-900: Microsoft Azure Fundamentals

Candidates for this exam should have foundational knowledge of cloud services and how those services are provided with Microsoft Azure. The exam is intended for candidates who are just beginning to work with cloud-based solutions and services or are new to Azure.

Azure Fundamentals exam is an opportunity to prove knowledge of cloud concepts, Azure services, Azure workloads, security and privacy in Azure, as well as Azure pricing and support. Candidates should be familiar with the general technology concepts, including concepts of networking, storage, compute, application support, and application development.

What is Azure Fundamentals?

Azure Fundamentals is a series of three learning paths that familiarize you with Azure and its many services and features.
Whether you're interested in compute, networking, or storage services; learning about cloud security best practices; or exploring governance and management options, think of Azure Fundamentals as your curated guide to Azure.
Azure Fundamentals includes interactive exercises that give you hands-on experience with Azure. Many exercises provide a temporary Azure portal environment called the sandbox, which allows you to practice creating cloud resources for free at your own pace.
Technical IT experience isn't required; however, having general IT knowledge will help you get the most from your learning experience.
Why should I take Azure Fundamentals?
If you're just beginning to work with the cloud, or if you already have cloud experience, Azure

Fundamentals provides you with everything you need to get started.
No matter your goals, Azure Fundamentals has something for you. You should take this course if you:
Have general interest in Azure or in the cloud
Want to earn official certification from Microsoft (AZ-900)

What is cloud computing?

Cloud computing is the delivery of computing services over the internet. Computing services include common IT infrastructure such as virtual machines, storage, databases, and networking. Cloud services also expand the traditional IT offerings to include things like Internet of Things (IoT), machine learning (ML), and artificial intelligence (AI). Because cloud computing uses the internet to deliver these services, it doesn't have to be constrained by physical infrastructure the same way that a traditional datacenter is. That means if you need to increase your IT infrastructure rapidly, you don't have to wait to build a new datacenter—you can use the cloud to rapidly expand your IT footprint.

Contents

CHAPTER I: Introduction to Azure

Microsoft Azure was officially launched on February 1, 2010, as Windows Azure. However, the platform's development began several years earlier, in 2006, under the codename "Project Red Dog." The goal of the project was to build a cloud-based operating system that would provide a scalable and reliable platform for hosting Microsoft's own online services.

Over time, Microsoft recognized the potential for Azure to be used by other businesses and began offering it as a commercial cloud computing platform. Azure initially offered a few core services, including virtual machines, cloud storage, and a content delivery network.

As the platform grew, Microsoft continued to add new services and features to Azure, including a wide range of compute options, analytics services, and developer tools. In 2014, Microsoft renamed the platform to Microsoft Azure to reflect its expanded capabilities beyond just Windows-based services.

Today, Microsoft Azure is one of the leading cloud computing platforms in the world, with a broad range of services and features that enable organizations to build, deploy, and manage applications and services in the cloud.

Azure is a cloud computing platform offered by Microsoft that provides a wide range of services and solutions for building, deploying, and managing applications and services through a global network of data centers. It offers a rich set of cloud-based services including virtual machines, databases, storage, networking, analytics, artificial intelligence (AI), machine learning, internet of things (IoT), and more.

Azure is designed to provide organizations with the flexibility and scalability to build, test, deploy, and manage applications and services on a global scale. It offers a variety of deployment models such as Infrastructure as a Service (IaaS), Platform as a Service (PaaS), and Software as a Service (SaaS) to suit different needs and workloads.

Azure Resource Manager is the central management layer that enables you to provision and manage resources across all Azure services. It provides a consistent and unified approach for creating, deploying, and managing resources, with a focus on ease of use, scalability, and security.

With Azure, you can easily integrate your existing IT infrastructure and applications with the cloud, providing a hybrid environment that enables you to leverage the benefits of both on-premises and cloud-based computing. Azure also offers a wide range of tools and services to help you manage your cloud resources, monitor performance, and troubleshoot issues, providing you with the visibility and control you need to run your business with confidence.

Azure responsibility model

- ➤ You may have heard of the shared responsibility model, but you may not understand what it means or how it impacts cloud computing.
- ➤ Start with a traditional corporate datacenter. The company is responsible for maintaining the physical space, ensuring security, and maintaining or replacing the servers if anything happens. The IT department is responsible for maintaining all the infrastructure and software needed to keep the datacenter up and running. They're also likely to be responsible for keeping all systems patched and on the correct version.
- ➤ With the shared responsibility model, these responsibilities get shared between the cloud provider and the consumer. Physical security, power, cooling, and network connectivity are the responsibility of the cloud provider. The consumer

isn't collocated with the datacenter, so it wouldn't make sense for the consumer to have any of those responsibilities.

➢ At the same time, the consumer is responsible for the data and information stored in the cloud. (You wouldn't want the cloud provider to be able to read your information.) The consumer is also responsible for access security, meaning you only give access to those who need it.

➢ Then, for some things, the responsibility depends on the situation. If you're using a cloud SQL database, the cloud provider would be responsible for maintaining the actual database. However, you're still responsible for the data that gets ingested into the database. If you deployed a virtual machine and installed an SQL database on it, you'd be responsible for database patches and updates, as well as maintaining the data and information stored in the database.

➢ With an on-premises datacenter, you're responsible for everything. With cloud computing, those responsibilities shift. The shared responsibility model is heavily tied into the cloud service types (covered later in this learning path): infrastructure as a service (IaaS), platform as a service (PaaS), and software as a service (SaaS). IaaS places the most responsibility on the consumer, with the cloud provider being responsible for the basics of physical security, power, and connectivity. On the other end of the spectrum, SaaS places most of the responsibility with the cloud provider. PaaS, being a middle ground between IaaS and SaaS, rests somewhere in the middle and evenly distributes responsibility between the cloud provider and the consumer.

You'll always be responsible for:

- The information and data stored in the cloud
- Devices that are allowed to connect to your cloud (cell phones, computers, and so on)
- The accounts and identities of the people, services, and devices within your organization
- The cloud provider is always responsible for:
- The physical datacenter
- The physical network
- The physical hosts
- Your service model will determine responsibility for things like:
- Operating systems
- Network controls
- Applications
- Identity and infrastructure

cloud models

What are cloud models? The cloud models define the deployment type of cloud resources. The three main cloud models are: private, public, and hybrid.

Private cloud

Let's start with a private cloud. A private cloud is, in some ways, the natural evolution from a corporate datacenter. It's a cloud (delivering IT services over the internet) that's used by a single entity. Private cloud provides much greater control for the company and its IT department. However, it also comes with greater cost and fewer of the benefits of a public cloud deployment. Finally, a private cloud may be hosted from your onsite datacenter. It may also be hosted in a dedicated datacenter offsite, potentially even by a third party that has dedicated that datacenter to your company.

Public cloud

A public cloud is built, controlled, and maintained by a third-party cloud provider. With a public cloud, anyone that wants to purchase cloud services can access and use resources. The general public availability is a key difference between public and private clouds.

Hybrid cloud

A hybrid cloud is a computing environment that uses both public and private clouds in an inter-connected environment. A hybrid cloud environment can be used to allow a private cloud to surge for increased, temporary demand by deploying public cloud resources. Hybrid cloud can be used to provide an extra layer of security. For example, users can flexibly choose which services to keep in public cloud and which to deploy to their private cloud infrastructure.

Multi-cloud

A fourth, and increasingly likely scenario is a multi-cloud scenario. In a multi-cloud scenario, you use multiple public cloud providers. Maybe you use different features from different cloud providers. Or maybe you started your cloud journey with one provider and are in the process of migrating to a different provider. Regardless, in a multi-cloud environment you deal with two (or more) public cloud providers and manage resources and security in both environments.

Azure Arc

Azure Arc is a set of technologies that helps manage your cloud environment. Azure Arc can help manage your cloud environment, whether it's a public cloud solely on Azure, a private cloud in your datacenter, a hybrid configuration, or even a multi-cloud environment running on multiple cloud providers at once.

Azure VMware Solution

What if you're already established with VMware in a private cloud environment but want to migrate to a public or hybrid cloud? Azure VMware Solution lets you run your VMware workloads in Azure with seamless integration and scalability.

consumption-based model

When comparing IT infrastructure models, there are two types of expenses to consider. Capital expenditure (CapEx) and operational expenditure (OpEx).

CapEx is typically a one-time, up-front expenditure to purchase or secure tangible resources. A new building, repaving the parking lot, building a datacenter, or buying a company vehicle are examples of CapEx.

In contrast, OpEx is spending money on services or products over time. Renting a convention center, leasing a company vehicle, or signing up for cloud services are all examples of OpEx.

Cloud computing falls under OpEx because cloud computing operates on a consumption-based model. With cloud computing, you don't pay for the physical infrastructure, the electricity, the security, or anything else associated with maintaining a datacenter. Instead, you pay for the IT resources you use. If you don't use any IT resources this month, you don't pay for any IT resources.

This **consumption-based model** has many benefits, including:

• No upfront costs.
• No need to purchase and manage costly infrastructure that users might not use to its fullest potential.
• The ability to pay for more resources when they're needed.
• The ability to stop paying for resources that are no longer needed.

With a traditional datacenter, you try to estimate the future resource needs. If you overestimate, you spend more on your datacenter than you need to and potentially waste money. If you underestimate, your datacenter will quickly reach capacity and your applications and services may suffer from decreased performance. Fixing an under-provisioned datacenter can take a long time. You may need to order, receive, and install more hardware. You'll also need to add power, cooling, and networking for the extra hardware.

In a cloud-based model, you don't have to worry about getting the resource needs just right. If you find that you need more virtual machines, you add more. If the demand drops and you don't need as many virtual machines, you remove machines as needed. Either way, you're only paying for the virtual machines that you use, not the "extra capacity" that the cloud provider has on hand.

Compare cloud pricing models

Cloud computing is the delivery of computing services over the internet by using a pay-as-you-go pricing model. You typically pay only for the cloud services you use, which helps you:

•	Plan and manage your operating costs.
•	Run your infrastructure more efficiently.
•	Scale as your business needs change.

To put it another way, cloud computing is a way to rent compute power and storage from someone else's datacenter. You can treat cloud resources like you would resources in your own datacenter. However, unlike in your own datacenter, when you're done using cloud resources, you give them back. You're billed only for what you use.

Instead of maintaining CPUs and storage in your datacenter, you rent them for the time that you need them. The cloud provider takes care of maintaining the underlying infrastructure for you. The cloud enables you to quickly solve your toughest business challenges and bring cutting-edge solutions to your users.

What does Azure offer?

With help from Azure, you have everything you need to build your next great solution. The following lists several of the benefits that Azure provides, so you can easily invent with purpose:

- **Be ready for the future**: Continuous innovation from Microsoft supports your development today and your product visions for tomorrow.
- **Build on your terms**: You have choices. With a commitment to open source, and support for all languages and frameworks, you can build how you want and deploy where you want.
- **Operate hybrid seamlessly**: On-premises, in the cloud, and at the edge, we'll meet you where you are. Integrate and manage your environments with tools and services designed for a hybrid cloud solution.
- **Trust your cloud**: Get security from the ground up, backed by a team of experts, and proactive compliance trusted by enterprises, governments, and startups.

What can I do with Azure?

Azure provides more than 100 services that enable you to do everything from running your existing applications on virtual machines to exploring new software paradigms, such as intelligent bots and mixed reality.

Many teams start exploring the cloud by moving their existing applications to virtual machines (VMs) that run in Azure. Migrating your existing apps to VMs is a good start, but the cloud is much more than a different place to run your VMs.

For example, Azure provides artificial intelligence (AI) and machine-learning (ML) services that can naturally communicate with your users through vision, hearing, and speech. It also provides storage solutions that dynamically grow to accommodate massive amounts of data. Azure services enable solutions that aren't feasible without the power of the cloud.

Azure provides a wide range of cloud-based services and solutions for building, deploying, and managing applications and services. Some of the core components of Azure include:

1. **Azure Resource Manager**: Azure Resource Manager (ARM) is the central management layer that enables you to provision and manage resources across all Azure services. It provides a consistent and unified approach for creating, deploying, and managing

resources, with a focus on ease of use, scalability, and security.

2. **Azure Virtual Machines**: Azure Virtual Machines (VMs) are on-demand, scalable computing resources that can be used to run applications and services in the cloud. VMs can be configured with various operating systems and can be customized to meet your specific needs.

3. Azure Storage: Azure Storage provides a scalable, secure, and highly available cloud-based storage solution for storing and managing data. It offers different storage types including Blob Storage, File Storage, and Queue Storage.

4. Azure Networking: Azure Networking provides a range of services for building and managing network infrastructure in the cloud. This includes virtual networks, load balancers, traffic managers, and VPN gateways.

5. **Azure App Service**: Azure App Service is a fully managed platform for building, deploying, and scaling web applications, mobile backends, and RESTful APIs. It supports various programming languages, including .NET, Java, Node.js, Python, and PHP.

6. **Azure SQL Database**: Azure SQL Database is a fully managed relational database service that provides high availability, scalability, and security for your applications. It supports various editions of SQL

Server, including Standard, Enterprise, and
Developer.

7. **Azure Active Directory**: Azure Active Directory
   (Azure AD) is a cloud-based identity and access
   management solution that provides authentication
   and authorization for your applications and services.
   It supports integration with various identity
   providers, including Microsoft accounts, social
   identities, and enterprise identities.

One real-world scenario for using the Azure cloud platform is
for a company that is looking to modernize their IT
infrastructure and move their applications and services to
the cloud. Here's an example of how they might use Azure:

1. First, they would assess their existing IT
   infrastructure and identify which applications and
   services are good candidates for migration to the
   cloud. They might start with low-risk applications
   and services, such as testing and development
   environments, and gradually move more critical
   applications and services to the cloud over time.
2. They would then create an Azure account and set up
   a subscription, choosing the pricing plan and options
   that best fit their needs. They might also choose to
   use Azure ExpressRoute to establish a dedicated,
   private connection between their on-premises data
   center and Azure.

3. Next, they would provision and configure Azure Virtual Machines to host their applications and services. They would choose the appropriate VM size and operating system, and set up networking and security to ensure that their applications and services are accessible and secure.

4. They would also set up Azure Storage to store and manage their data in the cloud. They might use Blob Storage to store unstructured data, such as documents and images, and Table Storage to store structured data, such as customer information and order details.

5. They would then deploy their applications and services to Azure using Azure Resource Manager templates. These templates would define the infrastructure and resources needed to run their applications and services, including Virtual Machines, Storage accounts, networking, and load balancing.

6. They would use Azure Monitor to monitor and manage their applications and services in the cloud. Azure Monitor provides real-time monitoring and alerts for application and infrastructure health, performance, and security, allowing them to quickly identify and resolve issues.

7. Finally, they would use Azure DevOps to manage their application development lifecycle in the cloud. Azure DevOps provides tools and services for source control, build and deployment, testing, and release

management, enabling them to develop and deploy applications and services quickly and efficiently.

By using the Azure cloud platform, this company would be able to modernize their IT infrastructure, reduce costs, increase scalability and agility, and improve application performance and security.

Azure Resource Manager

Azure Resource Manager (ARM) is the management layer that enables you to provision and manage resources in Azure. ARM provides a unified API, a consistent management portal, and a set of tools that enable you to deploy and manage your applications and services in the cloud.

With ARM, you can create, update, and delete Azure resources in a single, coordinated operation. This means you can deploy complex multi-tier applications and services with a single template that defines all the necessary resources and their dependencies.

ARM templates are JSON files that describe the infrastructure and resources that you want to deploy to Azure. They define resources such as virtual machines, storage accounts, networks, and load balancers, along with the properties and settings of those resources. You can author these templates manually or using tools like Visual Studio or the Azure Portal.

ARM also provides features like resource tagging, role-based access control (RBAC), and resource policies. Resource tagging enables you to label your resources with metadata, making it easier to manage and organize them. RBAC enables you to control who has access to your resources and what they can do with them. Resource policies enable you to enforce governance policies and standards across your Azure resources.

With ARM, you can deploy resources to Azure in a repeatable, automated, and predictable way. You can also manage and monitor your resources using a wide range of tools and services, including Azure Monitor, Azure Automation, and Azure Security Center. ARM provides a powerful and flexible platform for building, deploying, and managing your applications and services in Azure.

Azure Virtual Machines (VMs) and Azure Storage are two key components of the Azure platform. Here's an overview of each:

Azure Virtual Machines: Azure Virtual Machines are on-demand, scalable computing resources that can be used to run applications and services in the cloud. They provide a way to create and manage virtual machines in Azure, enabling you to deploy and run a variety of workloads, including Windows and Linux-based applications.

Some of the key features of Azure Virtual Machines include:

- **Flexibility and scalability**: You can choose from a wide range of VM sizes, from small VMs suitable for testing and development to large VMs with high-performance computing capabilities.
- **Pay-as-you-go pricing**: You only pay for what you use, with no upfront costs or termination fees.
- **Integration with other Azure services**: Azure Virtual Machines can be integrated with other Azure services, such as Azure Storage, Azure Networking, and Azure Active Directory, enabling you to build complex applications and services in the cloud.

Azure Storage: Azure Storage is a highly scalable, secure, and highly available cloud-based storage solution for storing and managing data in the cloud. It provides several types of storage options, including:

- **Blob Storage**: for unstructured data, such as text and binary data, that can be accessed from anywhere in the world over HTTP or HTTPS.
- **File Storage**: for managed file shares that can be accessed from multiple VMs or cloud services using the SMB protocol.
- **Queue Storage**: for storing and processing messages that can be accessed from anywhere in the world over HTTP or HTTPS.
- **Table Storage**: for storing structured NoSQL data, such as key-value pairs, that can be accessed from anywhere in the world over HTTP or HTTPS.

Some of the key features of Azure Storage include:

- **Scalability and flexibility**: Azure Storage scales to meet the needs of any workload, from small data sets to petabytes of data.
- **High availability**: Azure Storage provides built-in redundancy and replication to ensure that your data is always available.
- **Security**: Azure Storage provides multiple layers of security, including encryption at rest and in transit, and access control using Azure Active Directory.

Together, Azure Virtual Machines and Azure Storage provide a powerful platform for building, deploying, and managing applications and services in the cloud.

A retail company is looking to expand their online sales presence and improve their customer experience. They decide to migrate their e-commerce application to Azure and use several of the core components to build a scalable and reliable infrastructure. Here's how they might do it:

1. **Azure Resource Manager**: The retail company uses Azure Resource Manager to manage and deploy their infrastructure. They create a Resource Group to hold their resources and use templates to define their infrastructure as code.
2. **Azure Virtual Machines**: The company uses Azure Virtual Machines to run their e-commerce application. They create VMs for their web servers

and database servers, choosing the appropriate VM sizes and configuring the networking and security.

3. **Azure Storage**: To store their product images, customer information, and order data, the retail company uses Azure Storage. They use Blob Storage to store their product images and Table Storage to store their customer and order data.

4. **Azure Load Balancer**: To ensure high availability and reliability for their application, the company uses Azure Load Balancer. They configure the Load Balancer to distribute traffic evenly across their web servers, ensuring that customers can always access their e-commerce site.

5. **Azure Application Gateway**: To provide secure access to their e-commerce site, the company uses Azure Application Gateway. They configure the Application Gateway to provide SSL termination, web application firewall, and URL-based routing, ensuring that their site is protected against common web-based attacks.

6. **Azure Cosmos DB**: To provide real-time insights into their customer data, the retail company uses Azure Cosmos DB. They use Cosmos DB to store their customer behavior data and use Azure Stream Analytics to analyze the data in real-time, enabling them to personalize their customer experience and make data-driven decisions.

By using these Azure core components together, the retail company is able to build a scalable, reliable, and secure e-commerce infrastructure that can handle high volumes of traffic and provide a seamless customer experience.

Azure accounts

To create and use Azure services, you need an Azure subscription. When you're completing Learn modules, most of the time a temporary subscription is created for you, which runs in an environment called the Learn sandbox. When you're working with your own applications and business needs, you need to create an Azure account, and a subscription will be created for you. After you've created an Azure account, you're free to create additional subscriptions. For example, your company might use a single Azure account for your business and separate subscriptions for development, marketing, and sales departments. After you've created an Azure subscription, you can start creating Azure resources within each subscription.

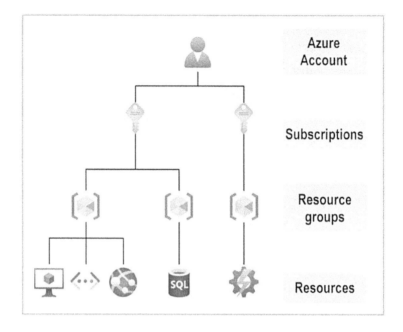

What is the Azure free account?

The Azure free account includes:

- Free access to popular Azure products for 12 months.
- A credit to use for the first 30 days.
- Access to more than 25 products that are always free.

The Azure free account is an excellent way for new users to get started and explore. To sign up, you need a phone number, a credit card, and a Microsoft or GitHub account. The credit card information is used for identity verification only. You won't be charged for any services until you upgrade to a paid subscription.

What is the Azure free student account?

The Azure free student account offer includes:

- Free access to certain Azure services for 12 months.
- A credit to use in the first 12 months.
- Free access to certain software developer tools.

The **Azure free student account** is an offer for students that gives $100 credit and free developer tools. Also, you can sign up without a credit card.

What is the Microsoft Learn sandbox?

Many of the Learn exercises use a technology called the sandbox, which creates a temporary subscription that's added to your Azure account. This temporary subscription allows you to create Azure resources during a Learn module. Learn automatically cleans up the temporary resources for you after you've completed the module.

When you're completing a Learn module, you're welcome to use your personal subscription to complete the exercises in a module. However, the sandbox is the preferred method to use because it allows you to create and test Azure resources at no cost to you.

Azure physical infrastructure

Throughout your journey with Microsoft Azure, you'll hear and use terms like Regions, Availability Zones, Resources, Subscriptions, and more. This module focuses on the core architectural components of Azure. The core architectural components of Azure may be broken down into two main groupings: the physical infrastructure, and the management infrastructure.

Physical infrastructure

The physical infrastructure for Azure starts with datacenters. Conceptually, the datacenters are the same as large corporate datacenters. They're facilities with resources arranged in racks, with dedicated power, cooling, and networking infrastructure.

As a global cloud provider, Azure has datacenters around the world. However, these individual datacenters aren't directly accessible. Datacenters are grouped into Azure Regions or Azure Availability Zones that are designed to help you achieve resiliency and reliability for your business-critical workloads.

Regions

A region is a geographical area on the planet that contains at least one, but potentially multiple datacenters that are nearby and networked together with a low-latency network. Azure intelligently assigns and controls the resources within each region to ensure workloads are appropriately balanced.

When you deploy a resource in Azure, you'll often need to choose the region where you want your resource deployed.

Availability Zones

Availability zones are physically separate datacenters within an Azure region. Each availability zone is made up of one or more datacenters equipped with independent power, cooling, and networking. An availability zone is set up to be an isolation boundary. If one zone goes down, the other continues working. Availability zones are connected through high-speed, private fiber-optic networks.

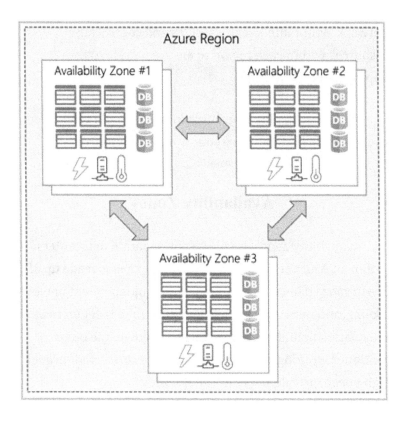

Use availability zones in your apps

You want to ensure your services and data are redundant so you can protect your information in case of failure. When you host your infrastructure, setting up your own redundancy requires that you create duplicate hardware environments. Azure can help make your app highly available through availability zones.

You can use availability zones to run mission-critical applications and build high-availability into your application architecture by co-locating your compute, storage, networking, and data resources within an availability zone and replicating in other availability zones. Keep in mind that there could be a cost to duplicating your services and transferring data between availability zones.

Availability zones are primarily for VMs, managed disks, load balancers, and SQL databases. Azure services that support availability zones fall into three categories:

- **Zonal services**: You pin the resource to a specific zone (for example, VMs, managed disks, IP addresses).
- **Zone-redundant services**: The platform replicates automatically across zones (for example, zone-redundant storage, SQL Database).
- **Non-regional services**: Services are always available from Azure geographies and are resilient to zone-wide outages as well as region-wide outages.

Even with the additional resiliency that availability zones provide, it's possible that an event could be so large that it impacts multiple availability zones in a single region. To provide even further resilience, Azure has Region Pairs.

Region pairs

Most Azure regions are paired with another region within the same geography (such as US, Europe, or Asia) at least 300 miles away. This approach allows for the replication of resources across a geography that helps reduce the likelihood of interruptions because of events such as natural disasters, civil unrest, power outages, or physical network outages that affect an entire region. For example, if a region in a pair was affected by a natural disaster, services would automatically fail over to the other region in its region pair.

Examples of region pairs in Azure are West US paired with East US and South-East Asia paired with East Asia. Because the pair of regions are directly connected and far enough apart to be isolated from regional disasters, you can use them to provide reliable services and data redundancy.

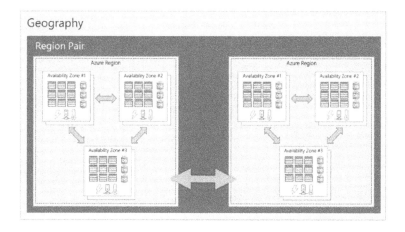

Sovereign Regions

In addition to regular regions, Azure also has sovereign regions. Sovereign regions are instances of Azure that are isolated from the main instance of Azure. You may need to use a sovereign region for compliance or legal purposes.

Azure sovereign regions include:

- US DoD Central, US Gov Virginia, US Gov Iowa and more: These regions are physical and logical network-isolated instances of Azure for U.S. government agencies and partners. These datacenters are operated by screened U.S. personnel and include additional compliance certifications.
- China East, China North, and more: These regions are available through a unique partnership between Microsoft and 21Vianet,

whereby Microsoft doesn't directly maintain the datacenters.

Azure storage accounts

A storage account provides a unique namespace for your Azure Storage data that's accessible from anywhere in the world over HTTP or HTTPS. Data in this account is secure, highly available, durable, and massively scalable.

When you create your storage account, you'll start by picking the storage account type. The type of account determines the storage services and redundancy options and has an impact on the use cases. Below is a list of redundancy options that will be covered later in this module:

- Locally redundant storage (LRS)
- Geo-redundant storage (GRS)
- Read-access geo-redundant storage (RA-GRS)
- Zone-redundant storage (ZRS)
- Geo-zone-redundant storage (GZRS)
- Read-access geo-zone-redundant storage (RA-GZRS)

Storage account endpoints

One of the benefits of using an Azure Storage Account is having a unique namespace in Azure for your data. In order to do this, every storage account in Azure must have a unique-in-Azure account name. The combination of the account name and the Azure Storage service endpoint forms the endpoints for your storage account.

When naming your storage account, keep these rules in mind:

- Storage account names must be between 3 and 24 characters in length and may contain numbers and lowercase letters only.
- Your storage account name must be unique within Azure. No two storage accounts can have the same name. This supports the ability to have a unique, accessible namespace in Azure.

Azure storage redundancy

Azure Storage always stores multiple copies of your data so that it's protected from planned and unplanned events such as transient hardware failures, network or power outages, and natural disasters. Redundancy ensures that your storage account meets its availability and durability targets even in the face of failures.

When deciding which redundancy option is best for your scenario, consider the tradeoffs between lower costs and higher availability. The factors that help determine which redundancy option you should choose include:

- How your data is replicated in the primary region.
- Whether your data is replicated to a second region that is geographically distant to the primary region, to protect against regional disasters.
- Whether your application requires read access to the replicated data in the secondary region if the primary region becomes unavailable.

Redundancy in the primary region

Data in an Azure Storage account is always replicated three times in the primary region. Azure Storage offers two options for how your data is replicated in the primary region, locally redundant storage (LRS) and zone-redundant storage (ZRS).

Locally redundant storage

Locally redundant storage (LRS) replicates your data three times within a single data center in the primary region. LRS provides at least 11 nines of durability (99.999999999%) of objects over a given year.

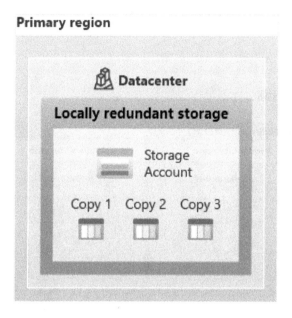

LRS is the lowest-cost redundancy option and offers the least durability compared to other options. LRS protects your data against server rack and drive failures. However, if a disaster such as fire or flooding occurs within the data center, all replicas of a storage account using LRS may be lost or unrecoverable. To mitigate this risk, Microsoft recommends using zone-redundant storage (ZRS), geo-redundant storage (GRS), or geo-zone-redundant storage (GZRS).

Zone-redundant storage

For Availability Zone-enabled Regions, zone-redundant storage (ZRS) replicates your Azure Storage data synchronously across three Azure availability zones in the primary region. ZRS offers durability for Azure Storage data objects of at least 12 nines (99.9999999999%) over a given year.

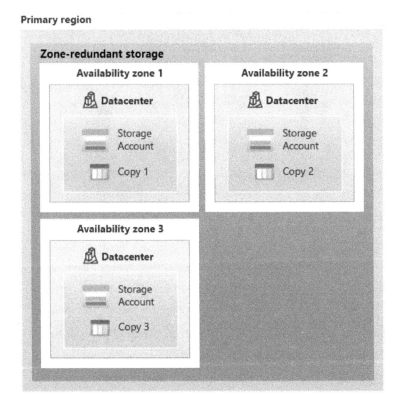

With ZRS, your data is still accessible for both read and write operations even if a zone becomes unavailable. No remounting of Azure file shares from the connected clients is required. If a zone becomes unavailable, Azure undertakes networking updates, such as DNS repointing. These updates may affect your application if you access data before the updates have completed.

Microsoft recommends using ZRS in the primary region for scenarios that require high availability. ZRS is also recommended for restricting replication of data within a country or region to meet data governance requirements.

Redundancy in a secondary region

For applications requiring high durability, you can choose to additionally copy the data in your storage account to a secondary region that is hundreds of miles away from the primary region. If the data in your storage account is copied to a secondary region, then your data is durable even in the event of a catastrophic failure that prevents the data in the primary region from being recovered.

When you create a storage account, you select the primary region for the account. The paired secondary region is based on Azure Region Pairs, and can't be changed.

Azure Storage offers two options for copying your data to a secondary region: geo-redundant storage (GRS) and geo-zone-redundant storage (GZRS). GRS is similar to running

LRS in two regions, and GZRS is similar to running ZRS in the primary region and LRS in the secondary region.

By default, data in the secondary region isn't available for read or write access unless there's a failover to the secondary region. If the primary region becomes unavailable, you can choose to fail over to the secondary region. After the failover has completed, the secondary region becomes the primary region, and you can again read and write data.

Important

Because data is replicated to the secondary region asynchronously, a failure that affects the primary region may result in data loss if the primary region can't be recovered. The interval between the most recent writes to the primary region and the last write to the secondary region is known as the recovery point objective (RPO). The RPO indicates the point in time to which data can be recovered. Azure Storage typically has an RPO of less than 15 minutes, although there's currently no SLA on how long it takes to replicate data to the secondary region.

Geo-redundant storage

GRS copies your data synchronously three times within a single physical location in the primary region using LRS. It then copies your data asynchronously to a single physical location in the secondary region (the region pair) using LRS.

GRS offers durability for Azure Storage data objects of at least 16 nines (99.99999999999999%) over a given year.

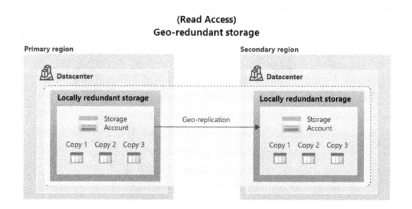

(Read Access)
Geo-redundant storage

Geo-zone-redundant storage

GZRS combines the high availability provided by redundancy across availability zones with protection from regional outages provided by geo-replication. Data in a GZRS storage account is copied across three Azure availability zones in the primary region (similar to ZRS) and is also replicated to a secondary geographic region, using LRS, for protection from regional disasters. Microsoft recommends using GZRS for applications requiring maximum consistency, durability, and availability, excellent performance, and resilience for disaster recovery.

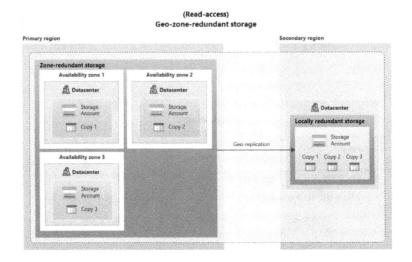

GZRS is designed to provide at least 16 nines (99.99999999999999%) of durability of objects over a given year.

Read access to data in the secondary region

Geo-redundant storage (with GRS or GZRS) replicates your data to another physical location in the secondary region to protect against regional outages. However, that data is available to be read only if the customer or Microsoft initiates a failover from the primary to secondary region. However, if you enable read access to the secondary region, your data is always available, even when the primary region is running optimally. For read access to the secondary region, enable read-access geo-redundant storage (RA-GRS) or read-access geo-zone-redundant storage (RA-GZRS).

Azure storage services

The Azure Storage platform includes the following data services:

- **Azure Blobs**: A massively scalable object store for text and binary data. Also includes support for big data analytics through Data Lake Storage Gen2.
- **Azure Files**: Managed file shares for cloud or on-premises deployments.
- **Azure Queues**: A messaging store for reliable messaging between application components.
- **Azure Disks**: Block-level storage volumes for Azure VMs.

Benefits of Azure Storage

Azure Storage services offer the following benefits for application developers and IT professionals:

- **Durable and highly available**. Redundancy ensures that your data is safe if transient hardware failures occur. You can also opt to replicate data across data centers or geographical regions for additional protection from local catastrophes or natural disasters. Data replicated in this way remains highly available if an unexpected outage occurs.
- **Secure**. All data written to an Azure storage account is encrypted by the service. Azure

Storage provides you with fine-grained control over who has access to your data.

- **Scalable**. Azure Storage is designed to be massively scalable to meet the data storage and performance needs of today's applications.
- **Managed**. Azure handles hardware maintenance, updates, and critical issues for you.
- **Accessible**. Data in Azure Storage is accessible from anywhere in the world over HTTP or HTTPS. Microsoft provides client libraries for Azure Storage in a variety of languages, including .NET, Java, Node.js, Python, PHP, Ruby, Go, and others, as well as a mature REST API. Azure Storage supports scripting in Azure PowerShell or Azure CLI. And the Azure portal and Azure Storage Explorer offer easy visual solutions for working with your data.

Blob storage

Azure Blob Storage is an object storage solution for the cloud. It can store massive amounts of data, such as text or binary data. Azure Blob Storage is unstructured, meaning that there are no restrictions on the kinds of data it can hold. Blob Storage can manage thousands of simultaneous uploads, massive amounts of video data, constantly growing log files, and can be reached from anywhere with an internet connection.

Blobs aren't limited to common file formats. A blob could contain gigabytes of binary data streamed from a scientific instrument, an encrypted message for another application, or data in a custom format for an app you're developing. One advantage of blob storage over disk storage is that it doesn't require developers to think about or manage disks. Data is uploaded as blobs, and Azure takes care of the physical storage needs.

Blob storage is ideal for:

- Serving images or documents directly to a browser.
- Storing files for distributed access.
- Streaming video and audio.
- Storing data for backup and restore, disaster recovery, and archiving.
- Storing data for analysis by an on-premises or Azure-hosted service.

Accessing blob storage

Objects in Blob storage can be accessed from anywhere in the world via HTTP or HTTPS. Users or client applications can access blobs via URLs, the Azure Storage REST API, Azure PowerShell, Azure CLI, or an Azure Storage client library. The storage client libraries are available for multiple languages, including .NET, Java, Node.js, Python, PHP, and Ruby.

Blob storage tiers

Data stored in the cloud can grow at an exponential pace. To manage costs for your expanding storage needs, it's helpful to organize your data based on attributes like frequency of access and planned retention period. Data stored in the cloud can be handled differently based on how it's generated, processed, and accessed over its lifetime. Some data is actively accessed and modified throughout its lifetime. Some data is accessed frequently early in its lifetime, with access dropping drastically as the data ages. Some data remains idle in the cloud and is rarely, if ever, accessed after it's stored. To accommodate these different access needs, Azure provides several access tiers, which you can use to balance your storage costs with your access needs.

Azure Storage offers different access tiers for your blob storage, helping you store object data in the most cost-effective manner. The available access tiers include:

- **Hot access tier**: Optimized for storing data that is accessed frequently (for example, images for your website).
- **Cool access tier**: Optimized for data that is infrequently accessed and stored for at least 30 days (for example, invoices for your customers).
- **Archive access tier**: Appropriate for data that is rarely accessed and stored for at least 180 days, with flexible latency requirements (for example, long-term backups).

The following considerations apply to the different access tiers:

- Only the hot and cool access tiers can be set at the account level. The archive access tier isn't available at the account level.
- Hot, cool, and archive tiers can be set at the blob level, during or after upload.
- Data in the cool access tier can tolerate slightly lower availability, but still requires high durability, retrieval latency, and throughput characteristics similar to hot data. For cool data, a slightly lower availability service-level agreement (SLA) and higher access costs compared to hot data are acceptable trade-offs for lower storage costs.
- Archive storage stores data offline and offers the lowest storage costs, but also the highest costs to rehydrate and access data.

Azure Files

Azure Files offers fully managed file shares in the cloud that are accessible via the industry standard Server Message Block (SMB) or Network File System (NFS) protocols. Azure Files file shares can be mounted concurrently by cloud or on-premises deployments. SMB Azure file shares are accessible from Windows, Linux, and macOS clients. NFS Azure Files shares are accessible from Linux or macOS clients. Additionally, SMB Azure file shares can be cached on

Windows Servers with Azure File Sync for fast access near where the data is being used.

Azure Files key benefits:

- **Shared access**: Azure file shares support the industry standard SMB and NFS protocols, meaning you can seamlessly replace your on-premises file shares with Azure file shares without worrying about application compatibility.
- **Fully managed**: Azure file shares can be created without the need to manage hardware or an OS. This means you don't have to deal with patching the server OS with critical security upgrades or replacing faulty hard disks.
- **Scripting and tooling**: PowerShell cmdlets and Azure CLI can be used to create, mount, and manage Azure file shares as part of the administration of Azure applications. You can create and manage Azure file shares using Azure portal and Azure Storage Explorer.
- **Resiliency**: Azure Files has been built from the ground up to always be available. Replacing on-premises file shares with Azure Files means you don't have to wake up in the middle of the night to deal with local power outages or network issues.

- **Familiar programmability**: Applications running in Azure can access data in the share via file system I/O APIs. Developers can therefore leverage their existing code and skills to migrate existing applications. In addition to System IO APIs, you can use Azure Storage Client Libraries or the Azure Storage REST API.

Queue storage

Azure Queue Storage is a service for storing large numbers of messages. Once stored, you can access the messages from anywhere in the world via authenticated calls using HTTP or HTTPS. A queue can contain as many messages as your storage account has room for (potentially millions). Each individual message can be up to 64 KB in size. Queues are commonly used to create a backlog of work to process asynchronously.

Queue storage can be combined with compute functions like Azure Functions to take an action when a message is received. For example, you want to perform an action after a customer uploads a form to your website. You could have the submit button on the website trigger a message to the Queue storage. Then, you could use Azure Functions to trigger an action once the message was received.

Disk storage

Disk storage, or Azure managed disks, are block-level storage volumes managed by Azure for use with Azure VMs. Conceptually, they're the same as a physical disk, but they're virtualized – offering greater resiliency and availability than a physical disk. With managed disks, all you have to do is provision the disk, and Azure will take care of the rest.

QUESTIONS AND ANSWERS

1. What is Microsoft Azure?

Microsoft Azure is a cloud computing platform and set of services provided by Microsoft. It allows individuals and organizations to build, deploy, and manage applications and services through a global network of data centers.

2. What are the benefits of using Microsoft Azure?

Some benefits of using Microsoft Azure include scalability, cost-effectiveness, flexibility, reliability, security, and accessibility.

3. What are the services provided by Microsoft Azure?

Microsoft Azure provides a wide range of services, including virtual machines, storage, databases, networking, analytics, artificial intelligence, Internet of Things (IoT), developer tools, security, and more.

4. What is a virtual machine in Microsoft Azure?

A virtual machine in Microsoft Azure is a virtualized computer system that runs on Microsoft's cloud platform. It allows users to create, deploy, and manage virtual machines on demand, providing the flexibility and scalability needed to meet changing business requirements.

5. What is Azure App Service?

Azure App Service is a fully managed platform that enables users to build, deploy, and scale web apps and APIs. It provides a wide range of features, including automatic scaling, continuous deployment, and integration with Azure DevOps.

6. What is Azure Storage?

Azure Storage is a cloud-based storage solution that provides users with a scalable, secure, and highly available storage platform. It allows users to store and retrieve data from anywhere in the world, using a variety of protocols and APIs.

7. What is Azure SQL Database?

Azure SQL Database is a cloud-based database service that provides users with a fully managed, scalable, and highly available relational database. It allows users to store and manage their data in the cloud, using a variety of tools and technologies.

8. What is Azure DevOps?

Azure DevOps is a set of development tools provided by Microsoft, including Azure Boards, Azure Repos, Azure Pipelines, Azure Test Plans, and Azure Artifacts. It enables users to plan, develop, test, and deploy applications and services in the cloud.

9. What is Azure Kubernetes Service?

Azure Kubernetes Service (AKS) is a fully managed service that enables users to deploy and manage containerized applications using Kubernetes. It provides a scalable, secure, and highly available platform for running containers in the cloud.

10. What is Azure Functions?

Azure Functions is a serverless computing service that enables users to run event-driven code without having to manage servers. It provides a scalable, cost-effective, and flexible platform for running code in the cloud.

QUESTIONS

1. What are some key features of Microsoft Azure?
2. How does Azure differ from other cloud computing platforms?

3. What are some common use cases for Microsoft Azure?
4. What are some of the security features available in Azure?
5. How does Azure support hybrid cloud deployments?
6. What is the pricing model for Microsoft Azure?
7. What certifications are available for Azure?
8. What is Azure Active Directory?
9. How does Azure support disaster recovery?
10. What is Azure Cosmos DB and how is it used?

CHAPTER II: Azure Networking

Azure networking refers to the networking features and services provided by Microsoft Azure, which is a cloud computing platform. Azure networking enables organizations to build and manage their network infrastructure in the cloud.

Azure networking includes a wide range of services, such as virtual networks (VNets), load balancing, VPN gateway, ExpressRoute, network security groups (NSGs), Azure Firewall, Azure DDoS Protection, and Network Watcher, among others. These services enable organizations to create isolated networks, connect virtual machines and services, establish secure connections with on-premises networks, filter network traffic, protect against DDoS attacks, monitor network performance, and more.

Azure networking also provides integration with other Azure services, such as Azure Active Directory, Azure Monitor, and Azure Security Center, to provide a comprehensive and cohesive approach to cloud networking.

Overall, Azure networking enables organizations to build and manage their network infrastructure in the cloud, with the flexibility, scalability, and security needed to support their applications and services.

Azure Virtual Machines

With Azure Virtual Machines (VMs), you can create and use VMs in the cloud. VMs provide infrastructure as a service (IaaS) in the form of a virtualized server and can be used in many ways. Just like a physical computer, you can customize all of the software running on your VM. VMs are an ideal choice when you need:

• Total control over the operating system (OS).
• The ability to run custom software.
• To use custom hosting configurations.

An Azure VM gives you the flexibility of virtualization without having to buy and maintain the physical hardware that runs the VM. However, as an IaaS offering, you still need to configure, update, and maintain the software that runs on the VM.

You can even create or use an already created image to rapidly provision VMs. You can create and provision a VM in minutes when you select a preconfigured VM image. An image is a template used to create a VM and may already include an OS and other software, like development tools or web hosting environments.

Scale VMs in Azure

You can run single VMs for testing, development, or minor tasks. Or you can group VMs together to provide high availability, scalability, and redundancy. Azure can also manage the grouping of VMs for you with features such as scale sets and availability sets.

Virtual machine scale sets

Virtual machine scale sets let you create and manage a group of identical, load-balanced VMs. If you simply created multiple VMs with the same purpose, you'd need to ensure they were all configured identically and then set up network routing parameters to ensure efficiency. You'd also have to monitor the utilization to determine if you need to increase or decrease the number of VMs.

Instead, with virtual machine scale sets, Azure automates most of that work. Scale sets allow you to centrally manage, configure, and update a large number of VMs in minutes. The number of VM instances can automatically increase or decrease in response to demand, or you can set it to scale based on a defined schedule. Virtual machine scale sets also automatically deploy a load balancer to make sure that your resources are being used efficiently. With virtual machine scale sets, you can build large-scale services for areas such as compute, big data, and container workloads.

Virtual machine availability sets

Virtual machine availability sets are another tool to help you build a more resilient, highly available environment. Availability sets are designed to ensure that VMs stagger updates and have varied power and network connectivity, preventing you from losing all your VMs with a single network or power failure.

Availability sets do this by grouping VMs in two ways: update domain and fault domain.

- **Update domain**: The update domain groups VMs that can be rebooted at the same time. This allows you to apply updates while knowing that only one update domain grouping will be offline at a time. All of the machines in one update domain will be updated. An update group going through the update process is given a 30-minute time to recover before maintenance on the next update domain starts.
- **Fault domain**: The fault domain groups your VMs by common power source and network switch. By default, an availability set will split your VMs across up to three fault domains. This helps protect against a physical power or networking failure by having VMs in different fault domains (thus being connected to different power and networking resources).

Best of all, there's no additional cost for configuring an availability set. You only pay for the VM instances you create.

Examples of when to use VMs

Some common examples or use cases for virtual machines include:

- **During testing and development**. VMs provide a quick and easy way to create different OS and application configurations. Test and development personnel can then easily delete the VMs when they no longer need them.
- **When running applications in the cloud**. The ability to run certain applications in the public cloud as opposed to creating a traditional infrastructure to run them can provide substantial economic benefits. For example, an application might need to handle fluctuations in demand. Shutting down VMs when you don't need them or quickly starting them up to meet a sudden increase in demand means you pay only for the resources you use.
- **When extending your datacenter to the cloud**: An organization can extend the capabilities of its own on-premises network by creating a virtual network in Azure and adding VMs to that virtual network. Applications like SharePoint can then run on an Azure VM instead of running locally. This arrangement makes it easier or less expensive to deploy than in an on-premises environment.

- **During disaster recovery**: As with running certain types of applications in the cloud and extending an on-premises network to the cloud, you can get significant cost savings by using an IaaS-based approach to disaster recovery. If a primary datacenter fails, you can create VMs running on Azure to run your critical applications and then shut them down when the primary datacenter becomes operational again.

Move to the cloud with VMs

VMs are also an excellent choice when you move from a physical server to the cloud (also known as lift and shift). You can create an image of the physical server and host it within a VM with little or no changes. Just like a physical on-premises server, you must maintain the VM: you're responsible for maintaining the installed OS and software.

VM Resources

When you provision a VM, you'll also have the chance to pick the resources that are associated with that VM, including:

• Size (purpose, number of processor cores, and amount of RAM)
• Storage disks (hard disk drives, solid state drives, etc.)

> - Networking (virtual network, public IP address, and port configuration)

Azure Virtual Desktop

Another type of virtual machine is the Azure Virtual Desktop. Azure Virtual Desktop is a desktop and application virtualization service that runs on the cloud. It enables you to use a cloud-hosted version of Windows from any location. Azure Virtual Desktop works across devices and operating systems, and works with apps that you can use to access remote desktops or most modern browsers.

Enhance security

Azure Virtual Desktop provides centralized security management for users' desktops with Azure Active Directory (Azure AD). You can enable multifactor authentication to secure user sign-ins. You can also secure access to data by assigning granular role-based access controls (RBACs) to users.

With Azure Virtual Desktop, the data and apps are separated from the local hardware. The actual desktop and apps are running in the cloud, meaning the risk of confidential data being left on a personal device is reduced. Additionally, user sessions are isolated in both single and multi-session environments.

Multi-session Windows 10 or Windows 11 deployment

Azure Virtual Desktop lets you use Windows 10 or Windows 11 Enterprise multi-session, the only Windows client-based operating system that enables multiple concurrent users on a single VM. Azure Virtual Desktop also provides a more consistent experience with broader application support compared to Windows Server-based operating systems.

Azure Containers

While virtual machines are an excellent way to reduce costs versus the investments that are necessary for physical hardware, they're still limited to a single operating system per virtual machine. If you want to run multiple instances of an application on a single host machine, containers are an excellent choice.

What are containers?

Containers are a virtualization environment. Much like running multiple virtual machines on a single physical host, you can run multiple containers on a single physical or virtual host. Unlike virtual machines, you don't manage the operating system for a container. Virtual machines appear to be an instance of an operating system that you can connect to and manage. Containers are lightweight and designed to be created, scaled out, and stopped dynamically. It's possible to create and deploy virtual machines as application demand increases, but containers are a lighter weight, more agile method. Containers are designed to allow you to respond to changes on demand. With containers, you can quickly restart if there's a crash or hardware interruption. One of the most popular container engines is Docker, which is supported by Azure.

Compare virtual machines to containers

The following video highlights several of the important differences between virtual machines and containers:

Azure Container Instances

Azure Container Instances offer the fastest and simplest way to run a container in Azure; without having to manage any virtual machines or adopt any additional services. Azure Container Instances are a platform as a service (PaaS) offering. Azure Container Instances allow you to upload your containers and then the service will run the containers for you.

Use containers in your solutions

Containers are often used to create solutions by using a microservice architecture. This architecture is where you break solutions into smaller, independent pieces. For example, you might split a website into a container hosting your front end, another hosting your back end, and a third for storage. This split allows you to separate portions of your app into logical sections that can be maintained, scaled, or updated independently.

Imagine your website back-end has reached capacity but the front end and storage aren't being stressed. With containers, you could scale the back end separately to improve performance. If something necessitated such a change, you could also choose to change the storage service or modify the front end without impacting any of the other components.

Azure Functions

Azure Functions is an event-driven, serverless compute option that doesn't require maintaining virtual machines or containers. If you build an app using VMs or containers, those resources have to be "running" in order for your app to function. With Azure Functions, an event wakes the function, alleviating the need to keep resources provisioned when there are no events.

Serverless computing in Azure

Benefits of Azure Functions

Using Azure Functions is ideal when you're only concerned about the code running your service and not about the underlying platform or infrastructure. Functions are commonly used when you need to perform work in response to an event (often via a REST request), timer, or message from another Azure service, and when that work can be completed quickly, within seconds or less.

Functions scale automatically based on demand, so they may be a good choice when demand is variable.

Azure Functions runs your code when it's triggered and automatically deallocates resources when the function is finished. In this model, you're only charged for the CPU time used while your function runs.

Functions can be either stateless or stateful. When they're stateless (the default), they behave as if they're restarted every time they respond to an event. When they're stateful (called Durable Functions), a context is passed through the function to track prior activity.

Functions are a key component of serverless computing. They're also a general compute platform for running any type of code. If the needs of the developer's app change, you can deploy the project in an environment that isn't serverless. This flexibility allows you to manage scaling, run on virtual networks, and even completely isolate the functions.

application hosting options

If you need to host your application on Azure, you might initially turn to a virtual machine (VM) or containers. Both VMs and containers provide excellent hosting solutions. VMs give you maximum control of the hosting environment and allow you to configure it exactly how you want. VMs also may be the most familiar hosting method if you're new to the cloud. Containers, with the ability to isolate and individually manage different aspects of the hosting solution, can also be a robust and compelling option.

There are other hosting options that you can use with Azure, including Azure App Service.

Azure App Service

App Service enables you to build and host web apps, background jobs, mobile back-ends, and RESTful APIs in the programming language of your choice without managing infrastructure. It offers automatic scaling and high availability. App Service supports Windows and Linux. It enables automated deployments from GitHub, Azure DevOps, or any Git repo to support a continuous deployment model.

Azure App Service is a robust hosting option that you can use to host your apps in Azure. Azure App Service lets you focus on building and maintaining your app, and Azure focuses on keeping the environment up and running.

Azure App Service is an HTTP-based service for hosting web applications, REST APIs, and mobile back ends. It supports multiple languages, including .NET, .NET Core, Java, Ruby, Node.js, PHP, or Python. It also supports both Windows and Linux environments.

Types of app services

With App Service, you can host most common app service styles like:

• Web apps
• API apps
• WebJobs
• Mobile apps

App Service handles most of the infrastructure decisions you deal with in hosting web-accessible apps:

• Deployment and management are integrated into the platform.
• Endpoints can be secured.
• Sites can be scaled quickly to handle high traffic loads.
• The built-in load balancing and traffic manager provide high availability.

All of these app styles are hosted in the same infrastructure and share these benefits. This flexibility makes App Service the ideal choice to host web-oriented applications.

Web apps

App Service includes full support for hosting web apps by using ASP.NET, ASP.NET Core, Java, Ruby, Node.js, PHP, or

Python. You can choose either Windows or Linux as the host operating system.

API apps

Much like hosting a website, you can build REST-based web APIs by using your choice of language and framework. You get full Swagger support and the ability to package and publish your API in Azure Marketplace. The produced apps can be consumed from any HTTP- or HTTPS-based client.

WebJobs

You can use the WebJobs feature to run a program (.exe, Java, PHP, Python, or Node.js) or script (.cmd, .bat, PowerShell, or Bash) in the same context as a web app, API app, or mobile app. They can be scheduled or run by a trigger. WebJobs are often used to run background tasks as part of your application logic.

Mobile apps

Use the Mobile Apps feature of App Service to quickly build a back end for iOS and Android apps. With just a few actions in the Azure portal, you can:

• Store mobile app data in a cloud-based SQL database.
• Authenticate customers against common social providers, such as MSA, Google, Twitter, and Facebook.

• Send push notifications.
• Execute custom back-end logic in C# or Node.js.

On the mobile app side, there's SDK support for native iOS and Android, Xamarin, and React native apps.

Azure Virtual Networking

Azure virtual networks and virtual subnets enable Azure resources, such as VMs, web apps, and databases, to communicate with each other, with users on the internet, and with your on-premises client computers. You can think of an Azure network as an extension of your on-premises network with resources that link other Azure resources.

Azure virtual networks provide the following key networking capabilities:

• Isolation and segmentation
• Internet communications
• Communicate between Azure resources
• Communicate with on-premises resources
• Route network traffic
• Filter network traffic
• Connect virtual networks

Azure virtual networking supports both public and private endpoints to enable communication between external or internal resources with other internal resources.

- Public endpoints have a public IP address and can be accessed from anywhere in the world.
- Private endpoints exist within a virtual network and have a private IP address from within the address space of that virtual network.

Isolation and segmentation

Azure virtual network allows you to create multiple isolated virtual networks. When you set up a virtual network, you define a private IP address space by using either public or private IP address ranges. The IP range only exists within the virtual network and isn't internet routable. You can divide that IP address space into subnets and allocate part of the defined address space to each named subnet.

For name resolution, you can use the name resolution service that's built into Azure. You also can configure the virtual network to use either an internal or an external DNS server.

Internet communications

You can enable incoming connections from the internet by assigning a public IP address to an Azure resource, or putting the resource behind a public load balancer.

Communicate between Azure resources

You'll want to enable Azure resources to communicate securely with each other. You can do that in one of two ways:

- **Virtual networks** can connect not only VMs but other Azure resources, such as the App Service Environment for Power Apps, Azure Kubernetes Service, and Azure virtual machine scale sets.
- **Service endpoints** can connect to other Azure resource types, such as Azure SQL databases and storage accounts. This approach enables you to link multiple Azure resources to virtual networks to improve security and provide optimal routing between resources.

Communicate with on-premises resources

Azure virtual networks enable you to link resources together in your on-premises environment and within your Azure subscription. In effect, you can create a network that spans both your local and cloud environments. There are three mechanisms for you to achieve this connectivity:

- **Point-to-site virtual private network** connections are from a computer outside your organization back into your corporate network. In this case, the client computer initiates an encrypted VPN connection to connect to the Azure virtual network.

- **Site-to-site virtual private networks** link your on-premises VPN device or gateway to the Azure VPN gateway in a virtual network. In effect, the devices in Azure can appear as being on the local network. The connection is encrypted and works over the internet.
- **Azure ExpressRoute** provides a dedicated private connectivity to Azure that doesn't travel over the internet. ExpressRoute is useful for environments where you need greater bandwidth and even higher levels of security.

Route network traffic

By default, Azure routes traffic between subnets on any connected virtual networks, on-premises networks, and the internet. You also can control routing and override those settings, as follows:

- **Route tables** allow you to define rules about how traffic should be directed. You can create custom route tables that control how packets are routed between subnets.
- **Border Gateway Protocol (BGP)** works with Azure VPN gateways, Azure Route Server, or Azure ExpressRoute to propagate on-premises BGP routes to Azure virtual networks.

Filter network traffic

Azure virtual networks enable you to filter traffic between subnets by using the following approaches:

- **Network security groups** are Azure resources that can contain multiple inbound and outbound security rules. You can define these rules to allow or block traffic, based on factors such as source and destination IP address, port, and protocol.
- **Network virtual appliances** are specialized VMs that can be compared to a hardened network appliance. A network virtual appliance carries out a particular network function, such as running a firewall or performing wide area network (WAN) optimization.

Connect virtual networks

You can link virtual networks together by using virtual network peering. Peering allows two virtual networks to connect directly to each other. Network traffic between peered networks is private, and travels on the Microsoft backbone network, never entering the public internet. Peering enables resources in each virtual network to communicate with each other. These virtual networks can be in separate regions, which allows you to create a global interconnected network through Azure.

User-defined routes (UDR) allow you to control the routing tables between subnets within a virtual network or between virtual networks. This allows for greater control over network traffic flow.

Azure provides a wide range of networking features that enable organizations to build and manage their network infrastructure in the cloud. Here are some of the key networking features of Azure:

1. **Virtual Networks (VNets):** VNets allow organizations to create isolated networks in Azure, with full control over IP address ranges, subnets, routing, and security. VNets can be used to connect virtual machines, services, and other resources within Azure or to extend on-premises networks into Azure.

2. **Load Balancing**: Azure provides multiple options for load balancing traffic across virtual machines and services, including Azure Load Balancer, Application Gateway, and Traffic Manager. These services can distribute traffic across multiple instances to improve performance and availability.

3. **VPN Gateway**: Azure VPN Gateway allows organizations to establish secure, site-to-site connections between Azure and on-premises networks, using industry-standard VPN protocols.

4. **ExpressRoute**: ExpressRoute provides a dedicated, private connection between Azure and on-premises

networks or colocation facilities, offering higher reliability, faster speeds, and lower latencies compared to public internet connections.

5. **Network Security Groups**: Network Security Groups (NSGs) enable organizations to filter network traffic based on source and destination IP address, port, and protocol. This helps organizations to enforce security policies and restrict access to resources.

6. **Azure Firewall**: Azure Firewall is a fully managed, cloud-native firewall service that provides network-level protection for Azure Virtual Network resources.

7. **Azure DDoS Protection:** Azure DDoS Protection is a service that provides advanced protection against Distributed Denial of Service (DDoS) attacks. It provides automatic detection and mitigation of DDoS attacks on Azure resources.

8. **Network Watcher**: Network Watcher is a network monitoring and diagnostic service that provides visibility into network performance and helps organizations to identify and troubleshoot networking issues.

Overall, these networking features of Azure provide organizations with the flexibility, scalability, and security needed to build and manage their network infrastructure in the cloud.

Azure networking provides organizations with control over subnets, IP addressing, and routing within their virtual network (VNet). Here is a brief overview of each:

1. **Subnets**: In Azure, a subnet is a range of IP addresses within a virtual network. Subnets can be used to segment resources within a VNet into smaller, isolated networks. This allows organizations to apply different security rules and network policies to different subnets.

2. **IP Addressing**: In Azure, IP addresses can be assigned to virtual machines, load balancers, and other resources within a virtual network. Azure supports both IPv4 and IPv6 addressing, and IP addresses can be assigned dynamically or statically. Organizations can also reserve IP addresses for specific resources to ensure that they remain consistent.

3. **Routing**: Azure networking provides organizations with control over the routing of network traffic within their virtual network. This includes the ability to define custom routing tables, control the flow of traffic between subnets, and establish connections between VNets using virtual network peering.

Overall, Azure networking enables organizations to design and implement complex network topologies within the cloud, while retaining control over subnets, IP addressing, and routing. This flexibility allows organizations to tailor their network infrastructure to meet their specific requirements, while ensuring security and reliability.

A large retail company with multiple stores across the country wants to migrate their Point of Sale (POS) system to the cloud to improve scalability and reduce costs. The POS system consists of virtual machines running on-premises, and the company wants to move these virtual machines to Azure.

Solution: The retail company can leverage Azure networking to support the migration of their POS system to the cloud. Here's how:

1. **Virtual Network**: The first step would be to create a virtual network (VNet) in Azure to house the virtual machines running the POS system. The VNet can be configured to provide an isolated network environment and can be split into subnets to segment the POS system components.

2. **VPN Gateway**: The company can use Azure VPN Gateway to create a secure, site-to-site connection between the on-premises data center and Azure. This will enable the virtual machines running the POS system to connect to on-premises resources such as Active Directory, SQL Server, and other backend systems.

3. **Load Balancing**: Azure Load Balancer can be used to distribute incoming traffic across multiple instances

of the virtual machines running the POS system. This will improve performance and ensure high availability of the POS system.

4. **Network Security Groups**: Network Security Groups (NSGs) can be used to apply access control lists (ACLs) to subnets and virtual machines. This will help the retail company to enforce security policies and restrict access to resources.

5. **Monitoring**: Azure Network Watcher can be used to monitor network performance, detect and diagnose network issues, and gain visibility into network traffic.

By leveraging Azure networking, the retail company can create a secure and reliable cloud environment for their POS system. This will provide them with the scalability and cost benefits of the cloud, while maintaining the security and reliability of their on-premises systems.

Azure networking features using the Azure portal or PowerShell:

1. Virtual Network (VNet):

Azure Portal:

- Navigate to the Azure portal and select "Create a Resource."
- Search for "Virtual Network" and select "Virtual Network."

- Fill in the required fields and select "Create" to create the VNet.

PowerShell:

- Use the command **New-AzVirtualNetwork** to create a new VNet.
- Specify the required parameters, such as the VNet name, address space, and subnet.
2. Load Balancing:

Azure Portal:

- Navigate to the Azure portal and select "Create a Resource."
- Search for "Load Balancer" and select "Load Balancer."
- Fill in the required fields and select "Create" to create the Load Balancer.

PowerShell:

- Use the command **New-AzLoadBalancer** to create a new Load Balancer.
- Specify the required parameters, such as the Load Balancer name, frontend IP configuration, and backend address pool.
3. Network Security Group (NSG):

Azure Portal:

- Navigate to the Azure portal and select "Create a Resource."
- Search for "Network Security Group" and select "Network Security Group."
- Fill in the required fields and select "Create" to create the NSG.

PowerShell:

- Use the command **New-AzNetworkSecurityGroup** to create a new NSG.
- Specify the required parameters, such as the NSG name, resource group, and location.
4. Virtual Network Peering:

Azure Portal:

- Navigate to the Azure portal and select the virtual network you want to peer with.
- Select "Peerings" and then select "Add."
- Fill in the required fields and select "Create" to create the peering.

PowerShell:

- Use the command **New-AzVirtualNetworkPeering** to create a new virtual network peering.
- Specify the required parameters, such as the peering name, virtual network name, and remote virtual network ID.

These are just a few examples of how to configure Azure networking features using the Azure portal or PowerShell. For more detailed instructions, you can refer to the Azure documentation or seek assistance from a certified Azure professional.

CHAPTER III: Managing Azure Resources

The management infrastructure includes Azure resources and resource groups, subscriptions, and accounts. Understanding the hierarchical organization will help you plan your projects and products within Azure.

Azure management infrastructure

The management infrastructure includes Azure resources and resource groups, subscriptions, and accounts. Understanding the hierarchical organization will help you plan your projects and products within Azure.

Azure resources and resource groups

A resource is the basic building block of Azure. Anything you create, provision, deploy, etc. is a resource. Virtual Machines (VMs), virtual networks, databases, cognitive services, etc. are all considered resources within Azure.

Resource groups are simply groupings of resources. When you create a resource, you're required to place it into a resource group. While a resource group can contain many resources, a single resource can only be in one resource group at a time. Some resources may be moved between resource groups, but when you move a resource to a new group, it will no longer be associated with the former group. Additionally, resource groups can't be nested, meaning you can't put resource group B inside of resource group A.

Resource groups provide a convenient way to group resources together. When you apply an action to a resource group, that action will apply to all the resources within the resource group. If you delete a resource group, all the resources will be deleted. If you grant or deny access to a resource group, you've granted or denied access to all the resources within the resource group.

When you're provisioning resources, it's good to think about the resource group structure that best suits your needs.

For example, if you're setting up a temporary dev environment, grouping all the resources together means you can deprovision all of the associated resources at once by deleting the resource group. If you're provisioning compute resources that will need three different access schemas, it may be best to group resources based on the access schema, and then assign access at the resource group level.

There aren't hard rules about how you use resource groups, so consider how to set up your resource groups to maximize their usefulness for you.

Azure subscriptions

In Azure, subscriptions are a unit of management, billing, and scale. Similar to how resource groups are a way to logically organize resources, subscriptions allow you to logically organize your resource groups and facilitate billing.

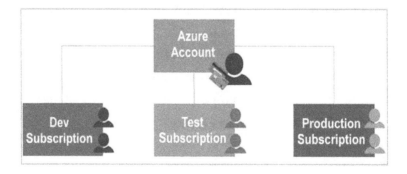

Using Azure requires an Azure subscription. A subscription provides you with authenticated and authorized access to Azure products and services. It also allows you to provision resources. An Azure subscription links to an Azure account, which is an identity in Azure Active Directory (Azure AD) or in a directory that Azure AD trusts.

An account can have multiple subscriptions, but it's only required to have one. In a multi-subscription account, you can use the subscriptions to configure different billing models and apply different access-management policies. You can use Azure subscriptions to define boundaries around Azure products, services, and resources. There are two types of subscription boundaries that you can use:

- **Billing boundary**: This subscription type determines how an Azure account is billed for using Azure. You can create multiple subscriptions for different types of billing requirements. Azure generates separate billing reports and invoices for each subscription so that you can organize and manage costs.
- **Access control boundary**: Azure applies access-management policies at the subscription level, and you can create separate subscriptions to reflect different organizational structures. An example is that within a business, you have different departments to which you apply distinct Azure subscription policies. This billing model allows you to

manage and control access to the resources that users provision with specific subscriptions.

Create additional Azure subscriptions

Similar to using resource groups to separate resources by function or access, you might want to create additional subscriptions for resource or billing management purposes. For example, you might choose to create additional subscriptions to separate:

- **Environments**: You can choose to create subscriptions to set up separate environments for development and testing, security, or to isolate data for compliance reasons. This design is particularly useful because resource access control occurs at the subscription level.
- **Organizational structures**: You can create subscriptions to reflect different organizational structures. For example, you could limit one team to lower-cost resources, while allowing the IT department a full range. This design allows you to manage and control access to the resources that users provision within each subscription.
- **Billing**: You can create additional subscriptions for billing purposes. Because costs are first aggregated at the subscription level, you might want to create subscriptions to manage and

track costs based on your needs. For instance, you might want to create one subscription for your production workloads and another subscription for your development and testing workloads.

Azure management groups

The final piece is the management group. Resources are gathered into resource groups, and resource groups are gathered into subscriptions. If you're just starting in Azure that might seem like enough hierarchy to keep things organized. But imagine if you're dealing with multiple applications, multiple development teams, in multiple geographies.

If you have many subscriptions, you might need a way to efficiently manage access, policies, and compliance for those subscriptions. Azure management groups provide a level of scope above subscriptions. You organize subscriptions into containers called management groups and apply governance conditions to the management groups. All subscriptions within a management group automatically inherit the conditions applied to the management group, the same way that resource groups inherit settings from subscriptions and resources inherit from resource groups. Management groups give you enterprise-grade management at a large scale, no matter what type of subscriptions you might have. Management groups can be nested.

Management group, subscriptions, and resource group hierarchy

You can build a flexible structure of management groups and subscriptions to organize your resources into a hierarchy for unified policy and access management. The following diagram shows an example of creating a hierarchy for governance by using management groups.

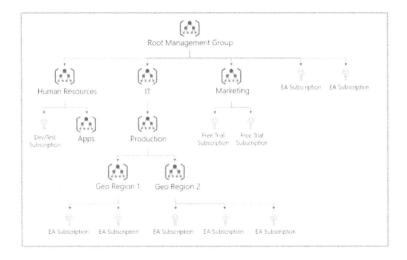

Some examples of how you could use management groups might be:

- **Create a hierarchy that applies a policy**. You could limit VM locations to the US West Region in a group called Production. This policy will inherit onto all the subscriptions that are descendants of that management group and will apply to all VMs under those subscriptions.

This security policy can't be altered by the resource or subscription owner, which allows for improved governance.

- **Provide user access to multiple subscriptions**. By moving multiple subscriptions under a management group, you can create one Azure role-based access control (Azure RBAC) assignment on the management group. Assigning Azure RBAC at the management group level means that all sub-management groups, subscriptions, resource groups, and resources underneath that management group would also inherit those permissions. One assignment on the management group can enable users to have access to everything they need instead of scripting Azure RBAC over different subscriptions.

Important facts about management groups:

- 10,000 management groups can be supported in a single directory.
- A management group tree can support up to six levels of depth. This limit doesn't include the root level or the subscription level.
- Each management group and subscription can support only one parent.

Managing Azure resources involves performing tasks such as creating, updating, deleting, and monitoring Azure resources. Here are some common methods for managing Azure resources:

1. **Azure Portal**: The Azure Portal is a web-based interface that allows you to manage Azure resources visually. You can use the portal to create and manage resources, view metrics and logs, and configure alerts.

2. **Azure PowerShell**: Azure PowerShell is a command-line interface that allows you to manage Azure resources using PowerShell commands. You can use Azure PowerShell to create and manage resources, automate tasks, and deploy resources.

3. **Azure CLI**: Azure CLI is a cross-platform command-line interface that allows you to manage Azure resources using commands. You can use Azure CLI to create and manage resources, automate tasks, and deploy resources.

4. **Azure REST API**: Azure REST API allows you to manage Azure resources programmatically. You can use any programming language that supports HTTP requests to interact with the REST API and perform tasks such as creating and managing resources.

5. **Azure Resource Manager (ARM) templates:** ARM templates allow you to define and deploy Azure resources using JSON files. You can use ARM

templates to automate the deployment of resources, create consistent environments, and manage complex deployments.

6. Azure DevOps: Azure DevOps is a suite of services that allows you to manage the entire software development lifecycle. You can use Azure DevOps to plan, develop, test, and deploy applications to Azure.

Creating and managing resource groups:

1. Azure Portal:
- Navigate to the Azure portal and select "Resource groups" from the left-hand menu.
- Click on the "Add" button and fill in the required fields such as the name, subscription, and region.
- Select "Review + create" and then click "Create" to create the resource group.
2. Azure PowerShell:
- Use the command **New-AzResourceGroup** to create a new resource group.
- Specify the required parameters, such as the resource group name, location, and subscription ID.
- Use the command **Get-AzResourceGroup** to retrieve information about an existing resource group.
- Use the command **Remove-AzResourceGroup** to delete a resource group.

Deploying resources using templates:

1. **Azure Portal**:

- Navigate to the Azure portal and select "Create a resource."
- Search for the resource you want to deploy and select it.
- Click on the "Create" button to begin the deployment process.
- Fill in the required fields and select "Review + create" to review the deployment settings.
- Select "Create" to deploy the resource.

2. **Azure PowerShell**:

- Use the command **New-AzResourceGroupDeployment** to deploy resources from an Azure Resource Manager template.
- Specify the required parameters, such as the resource group name, location, and template file path.
- Use the command **Get-AzResourceGroupDeployment** to retrieve information about an existing deployment.
- Use the command **Remove-AzResourceGroupDeployment** to delete a deployment.

Using templates to deploy resources provides the ability to define and deploy resources repeatedly and consistently, and Azure provides various templates and resource options that you can use to deploy and manage resources efficiently.

Monitoring resource usage and performance:

1. **Azure Monitor**:
   - Azure Monitor provides a centralized platform for monitoring and analyzing Azure resources.
   - You can use Azure Monitor to monitor the performance and availability of your applications and infrastructure, identify issues and diagnose problems, and configure alerts and notifications.
2. **Azure Advisor**:
   - Azure Advisor provides recommendations based on your usage and configurations to optimize your resources and improve their efficiency and performance.
   - It provides recommendations on areas such as high availability, security, performance, and cost.
3. Azure Metrics:
   - Azure Metrics provides data on the performance of your Azure resources.
   - You can use Azure Metrics to monitor various metrics such as CPU usage, memory usage, network traffic, and disk usage.

Tagging:

- Tagging allows you to organize and categorize resources in Azure.
- You can use tags to identify the owner of the resource, the environment it belongs to, or any other relevant metadata.

RBAC:

- Role-Based Access Control (RBAC) allows you to grant permissions to users, groups, or applications to access Azure resources.
- You can use RBAC to control access to resources based on roles such as owner, contributor, or reader.

Azure Policies:

- Azure Policies allows you to enforce governance in your Azure environment.
- You can use Azure Policies to define and enforce rules that apply to your resources such as tagging requirements, access controls, or compliance standards.

QUESTIONS AND ANSWERS

What is Azure Active Directory? A: Azure Active Directory (Azure AD) is a cloud-based identity and access management service that provides authentication and authorization services for applications and resources across Azure and other Microsoft services.

Q: How does Azure AD protect user accounts? A: Azure AD uses multiple layers of security to protect user accounts, including strong password policies, multi-factor authentication, conditional access policies, and risk-based authentication.

Q: What is Azure Security Center? A: Azure Security Center is a unified security management solution that provides threat protection for workloads running in Azure, as well as on-premises and in other clouds. It uses advanced analytics and machine learning to detect and respond to security threats.

Q: How does Azure Security Center protect resources? A: Azure Security Center provides continuous security monitoring and threat protection for Azure resources, including virtual machines, network security groups, and storage accounts. It also provides security recommendations and alerts for potential vulnerabilities and misconfigurations.

Q: What is Azure Key Vault? A: Azure Key Vault is a cloud-based service that allows you to securely store and manage cryptographic keys, secrets, and certificates. It provides centralized management of secrets and keys used in applications and services.

Q: How does Azure Key Vault protect secrets and keys? A: Azure Key Vault uses hardware security modules (HSMs) to protect cryptographic keys and secrets. It also provides role-based access control, auditing, and monitoring to ensure that secrets and keys are accessed only by authorized users and applications.

CHAPTER IV: Azure Security and Identity

Security and identity features are critical components of any cloud environment. Azure provides several security and identity features to help secure and manage resources effectively. Some of these features include:

1. **Azure Active Directory (AD):**
    - Azure AD is a cloud-based identity and access management service that allows you to manage user identities and access to resources in Azure and other Microsoft services.
    - You can use Azure AD to authenticate and authorize users, manage roles and access control, and enable single sign-on (SSO) across applications and devices.
2. **Azure Security Center:**
    - Azure Security Center provides a centralized platform for monitoring and managing the security of Azure resources.
    - You can use **Azure Security Center** to monitor security alerts and recommendations, detect and respond to threats, and ensure compliance with industry standards.
3. **Azure Firewall:**
    - Azure Firewall is a cloud-based firewall service that allows you to secure your virtual network and protect your resources from unauthorized access.

- You can use Azure Firewall to filter network traffic, create network rules, and control outbound internet access.

4. **Azure DDoS Protection:**

- Azure DDoS Protection provides protection against Distributed Denial of Service (DDoS) attacks.
- You can use Azure DDoS Protection to detect and mitigate DDoS attacks, ensure high availability, and maintain business continuity.

5. **Azure Key Vault:**

- Azure Key Vault is a cloud-based service that allows you to store and manage cryptographic keys, certificates, and secrets.
- You can use Azure Key Vault to protect your data and applications by storing and managing sensitive information such as passwords, connection strings, and encryption keys.

A company has recently migrated its IT infrastructure to Azure and is looking to improve its identity and access management capabilities. The company has multiple applications and services that require authentication and authorization, and it wants to centralize the management of user identities and access to resources.

Solution: The company can leverage Azure AD to manage user identities and access to resources in Azure and other

Microsoft services. Here are the steps that the company can follow:

1. **Set up Azure AD**: The company can create an Azure AD tenant and configure its settings, such as authentication methods, user attributes, and access policies.

2. **Configure applications and services**: The company can configure its applications and services to use Azure AD for authentication and authorization. This can be done by adding the applications and services to Azure AD and configuring their settings, such as access control and user roles.

3. **Add users and groups**: The company can add its users and groups to Azure AD and assign them appropriate roles and access policies. This can be done manually or by syncing the on-premises Active Directory with Azure AD.

4. **Enable single sign-on**: The company can enable single sign-on (SSO) across its applications and services by configuring Azure AD to use SSO protocols such as SAML or OpenID Connect.

5. **Monitor and manage access**: The company can use Azure AD to monitor and manage user access to resources. This can be done by configuring access policies, setting up multi-factor authentication (MFA), and using Azure AD's reporting and auditing capabilities.

By leveraging Azure AD, the company can centralize the management of user identities and access to resources, improve its security posture, and streamline its identity and access management processes. Azure AD provides a scalable and flexible solution that can meet the company's evolving identity and access management needs.

Azure Security Center and Azure Key Vault are two important security and compliance services offered by Azure. Here's an overview of each service:

1. **Azure Security Center**: Azure Security Center is a unified infrastructure security management system that provides threat protection across your hybrid cloud workloads. It provides a centralized platform for monitoring and managing the security of Azure resources. Azure Security Center continuously monitors and analyzes security data from various sources, including Azure resources, network traffic, and endpoint protection solutions.

Azure Security Center offers the following features:

- Security assessments and recommendations for Azure resources
- Threat detection and response for cloud and on-premises workloads
- Integration with third-party security solutions

- Compliance assessments and reporting for industry standards and regulations
- Secure score to measure your security posture
2. **Azure Key Vault**: Azure Key Vault is a cloud-based service that allows you to store and manage cryptographic keys, certificates, and secrets. Azure Key Vault provides a secure and centralized location for key management and storage.

Azure Key Vault offers the following features:

• Secure storage of cryptographic keys and secrets
• Management of certificates
• Integration with Azure services and applications
• Key lifecycle management, including key rotation and backup
• Access control and permission management

Identity management, access control, and data protection are critical components of a comprehensive security strategy in Azure. Here's an overview of each area:

1. **Identity management:** Identity management involves the management of user identities and access to resources. Azure Active Directory (AD) is a cloud-based identity and access management service that provides a centralized platform for managing user identities and access to resources. Azure AD

enables single sign-on (SSO) across cloud and on-premises applications, and supports multi-factor authentication (MFA) to enhance security.

2. **Access control**: Access control involves the management of access to resources based on user roles and permissions. Azure provides a variety of access control mechanisms, including role-based access control (RBAC), Azure AD conditional access, and Azure AD Privileged Identity Management (PIM). RBAC allows you to define roles and permissions for users and groups, while Azure AD conditional access allows you to control access based on conditions such as user location and device status. Azure AD PIM enables just-in-time access to high-privileged roles, reducing the risk of unauthorized access.

3. **Data protection**: Data protection involves the management of data security, confidentiality, and integrity. Azure provides a variety of data protection mechanisms, including encryption, data classification, and data loss prevention (DLP). Azure Storage Service Encryption (SSE) and Azure Disk Encryption (ADE) provide encryption for data at rest, while Azure Key Vault enables secure storage and management of cryptographic keys. Azure Information Protection (AIP) provides data classification and labeling, as well as DLP capabilities to prevent data leakage.

Azure's identity management, access control, and data protection features to secure your Azure environment, you can follow these general steps:

1. **Identity management**:

• Set up Azure AD and sync your on-premises identities to Azure AD.
• Configure single sign-on (SSO) for your cloud and on-premises applications.
• Implement multi-factor authentication (MFA) for added security.
• Use Azure AD Privileged Identity Management (PIM) to control access to high-privileged roles.

2. **Access control**:

• Define roles and permissions using role-based access control (RBAC).
• Use Azure AD conditional access to control access based on user location and device status.
• Use Azure AD Privileged Identity Management (PIM) to enable just-in-time access to high-privileged roles.

3. Data protection:

• Use Azure Storage Service Encryption (SSE) and Azure Disk Encryption (ADE) to encrypt data at rest.
• Use Azure Key Vault to securely store and manage cryptographic keys.
• Use Azure Information Protection (AIP) to classify and label sensitive data, and implement data loss prevention (DLP) policies to prevent data leakage.

In addition to these general steps, here are some specific tips for using these features to secure your Azure environment:

• Regularly review and update your RBAC roles and permissions to ensure that access is appropriate and up-to-date.
• Monitor Azure AD sign-ins and audit logs for unusual activity, and investigate any suspicious behavior.
• Implement Azure AD Identity Protection to detect and prevent identity-based attacks.
• Use Azure Security Center to monitor the security of your Azure resources and receive recommendations for improving security posture.
• Regularly review and update your Azure policies to ensure that your environment is compliant with industry standards and regulations.

By following these steps and leveraging Azure's identity management, access control, and data protection features, you can help ensure that your Azure environment is secure and compliant with industry standards and regulations.

A multinational company has thousands of employees across multiple locations and needs to provide them with secure access to the company's cloud and on-premises applications. The company wants to ensure that only authorized employees can access company resources, and that access is granted based on employees' roles and responsibilities. The company also wants to implement multi-factor authentication (MFA) to enhance security.

To address these requirements, the company can use Azure Active Directory (AD) as its identity management solution. The company can sync its on-premises identities to Azure AD and use Azure AD Connect to manage the synchronization process. The company can then configure single sign-on (SSO) for its cloud and on-premises applications, allowing employees to sign in once and access all their authorized applications.

To ensure that only authorized employees can access company resources, the company can define roles and permissions using Azure AD role-based access control (RBAC). The company can also use Azure AD conditional access to control access based on user location and device status, and use Azure AD Privileged Identity Management (PIM) to control access to high-privileged roles.

To enhance security, the company can implement MFA for all its employees using Azure AD conditional access. Employees can be required to use MFA when accessing company resources from outside the corporate network or from devices that are not managed by the company. The company can also use Azure AD Identity Protection to detect and prevent identity-based attacks.

By leveraging Azure identity management features, the company can provide its employees with secure access to company resources while ensuring that access is granted based on employees' roles and responsibilities. The company can also enhance security by implementing MFA and detecting and preventing identity-based attacks.

CHAPTER V: Azure Solutions

Azure provides a wide range of solutions for various use cases. Here are some of the most common Azure solutions and their use cases:

1. **Web Applications**: Azure App Service is a fully managed platform for building, deploying, and scaling web applications. It supports various programming languages such as .NET, Java, PHP, Node.js, and Python, making it ideal for hosting web applications built with different technologies. Azure App Service also provides features such as automatic scaling, load balancing, and integration with other Azure services.

2. **Databases**: Azure offers various database solutions such as Azure SQL Database, Azure Cosmos DB, Azure Database for MySQL, and Azure Database for PostgreSQL. These solutions provide fully managed database services with built-in high availability, scalability, and security features. They are suitable for hosting different types of databases, including relational, NoSQL, and open source databases.

3. **DevOps**: Azure DevOps is a comprehensive set of tools and services for managing the entire DevOps lifecycle. It includes features such as version control, continuous integration and delivery, testing, and deployment. With Azure DevOps, you can automate your build and release processes, collaborate with your team, and manage your code and artifacts in a secure and scalable environment.

4. **Analytics**: Azure provides various analytics solutions such as Azure Synapse Analytics, Azure Stream Analytics, and Azure Data Lake Storage. These solutions enable you to ingest, store, process, and analyze large volumes of data in real-time or batch mode. They support various data types such as structured, semi-structured, and unstructured data and provide powerful tools for data exploration, visualization, and machine learning.

5. **Internet of Things (IoT):** Azure IoT Hub is a fully managed service for connecting, monitoring, and managing IoT devices at scale. It provides features such as device management, data ingestion, real-time monitoring, and integration with other Azure services. With Azure IoT Hub, you can build and deploy IoT solutions with ease and leverage the power of the cloud for processing and analyzing IoT data.

These are just some of the common Azure solutions and use cases. Azure provides a wide range of services for different scenarios and industries, making it a versatile and scalable platform for building, deploying, and managing applications and services in the cloud.

Azure App Service and Azure **SQL Database** are two popular services offered by Azure.

Azure App Service is a fully managed platform for building, deploying, and scaling web applications. It supports various programming languages such as .NET, Java, PHP, Node.js, and Python, making it ideal for hosting web applications built with different technologies. Azure App Service also provides features such as automatic scaling, load balancing, and integration with other Azure services.

Azure SQL Database is a fully managed relational database service provided by Azure. It is based on Microsoft SQL Server engine and provides a scalable and highly available database solution with built-in security and compliance features. Azure SQL Database supports various database engines such as SQL Server, MySQL, and PostgreSQL, making it a versatile and flexible solution for different types of databases.

Together, Azure App Service and Azure SQL Database provide a powerful and scalable solution for building and deploying web applications with a reliable and secure backend. With Azure App Service, you can easily deploy and manage your web applications, while Azure SQL Database provides a highly available and scalable database backend that supports various database engines and provides built-in security and compliance features.

1. **Architecture**: When architecting your solution using Azure App Service and Azure SQL Database, it's important to consider factors such as performance, scalability, availability, and security. You can design your architecture using best practices such as using load balancers, auto-scaling, and multi-region deployment to achieve high availability and performance. You can also leverage Azure security features such as Azure Active Directory, Azure Security Center, and Azure Key Vault to enhance the security of your solution.

2. **Deployment**: To deploy your solution, you can use Azure DevOps, Azure CLI, or Azure Portal. Azure DevOps provides a comprehensive set of tools and services for managing the entire DevOps lifecycle, including version control, continuous integration and delivery, testing, and deployment. Azure CLI is a command-line tool that enables you to manage Azure resources and automate deployment tasks. Azure Portal is a web-based management console that enables you to deploy and manage resources in a visual and intuitive way.

3. **Management**: To manage your solution, you can use Azure monitoring and alerting services such as Azure Monitor and Azure Log Analytics. Azure Monitor

provides a centralized monitoring and alerting solution for all your Azure resources, including Azure App Service and Azure SQL Database. It enables you to monitor performance metrics, logs, and events, and set up alerts based on predefined or custom criteria. Azure Log Analytics provides a centralized log management solution that enables you to collect, store, and analyze logs from different sources, including Azure App Service and Azure SQL Database. It enables you to troubleshoot issues and gain insights into the performance and usage of your solution.

4. **Best Practices**: Here are some best practices for architecting, deploying, and managing Azure App Service and Azure SQL Database:

• Use Azure Resource Manager templates for deploying and managing resources in a consistent and repeatable way.
• Use Azure Traffic Manager or Azure Front Door to distribute traffic across multiple regions for high availability and performance.
• Use Azure Backup and Azure Site Recovery to protect your data and applications from disasters and outages.
• Use Azure Application Gateway for web application firewall and load balancing.

> • Use Azure Advisor to get recommendations for optimizing your Azure resources and improving their performance, security, and cost efficiency.

By following these best practices and using Azure services and tools for architecture, deployment, and management, you can build a scalable, reliable, and secure solution using Azure App Service and Azure SQL Database.

A company wants to migrate their on-premises web application to the cloud to improve its scalability, availability, and security. The web application is built using .NET and uses Microsoft SQL Server as its backend database. The company wants to use Azure solutions to deploy and manage the web application in the cloud.

Solution:

1. **Architecture**: To architect the solution, the company decides to use Azure App Service to host the web application and Azure SQL Database to host the database backend. They use Azure Traffic Manager to distribute traffic across multiple regions for high availability and performance. They also use Azure Application Gateway for web application firewall and load balancing.
2. **Deployment**: To deploy the solution, the company uses Azure DevOps to automate the deployment

process. They create a CI/CD pipeline that includes version control, build, test, and deployment steps. They use Azure Resource Manager templates to deploy the infrastructure and the application code. They also use Azure CLI to automate the deployment tasks.

3. **Management**: To manage the solution, the company uses Azure Monitor and Azure Log Analytics for monitoring and alerting. They set up alerts based on predefined and custom criteria to notify them of any issues with the web application or the database. They use Azure Advisor to get recommendations for optimizing the performance, security, and cost efficiency of their Azure resources.

4. **Best Practices**: The company follows best practices for deploying and managing Azure solutions, such as using Azure Resource Manager templates, automating the deployment process, using Azure Traffic Manager and Azure Application Gateway for high availability and performance, and using Azure Monitor and Azure Log Analytics for monitoring and alerting.

By using Azure solutions, the company is able to migrate their web application to the cloud with minimal downtime and improve its scalability, availability, and security. They are able to leverage the benefits of Azure App Service and Azure SQL Database to provide a reliable and scalable solution for their customers. They also benefit from the automation and monitoring capabilities of Azure DevOps, Azure Resource Manager, Azure Monitor, and Azure Log Analytics, which enable them to manage their solution more efficiently and effectively.

Azure shifts development costs from the capital expense (CapEx) of building out and maintaining infrastructure and facilities to an operational expense (OpEx) of renting infrastructure as you need it, whether it's compute, storage, networking, and so on.

That OpEx cost can be impacted by many factors. Some of the impacting factors are:

• Resource type
• Consumption
• Maintenance
• Geography
• Subscription type
• Azure Marketplace

Resource type

A number of factors influence the cost of Azure resources. The type of resources, the settings for the resource, and the Azure region will all have an impact on how much a resource costs. When you provision an Azure resource, Azure creates metered instances for that resource. The meters track the resources' usage and generate a usage record that is used to calculate your bill.

Examples

With a storage account, you specify a type such as blob, a performance tier, an access tier, redundancy settings, and a region. Creating the same storage account in different regions may show different costs and changing any of the settings may also impact the price.

Blob storage

Enable SFTP

    To enable SFTP 'hierarchical namespace' must be enabled.

Enable network file system v3

    To enable NFS v3 'hierarchical namespace' must be enabled. Learn more about NFS v3

Allow cross-tenant replication ☑

Access tier
    ◉ Hot: Frequently accessed data and day-to-day usage scenarios
    ○ Cool: Infrequently accessed data and backup scenarios

With a virtual machine (VM), you may have to consider licensing for the operating system or other software, the processor and number of cores for the VM, the attached storage, and the network interface. Just like with storage, provisioning the same virtual machine in different regions may result in different costs.

Create a virtual machine ...

Basics Disks Networking Management Advanced Tags Review + create

Create a virtual machine that runs Linux or Windows. Select an image from Azure marketplace or use your own customized image. Complete the Basics tab then Review + create to provision a virtual machine with default parameters or review each tab for full customization. Learn more ⓘ

Project details

Select the subscription to manage deployed resources and costs. Use resource groups like folders to organize and manage all your resources.

Subscription * ⓘ	Visual Studio Enterprise Subscription ⌄
Resource group * ⓘ	[New] Resource group ⌄
	Create new

Instance details

Virtual machine name * ⓘ	
Region * ⓘ	Your recently used sizes
Availability options ⓘ	Standard_D2s_v3 - 2 vcpus, 8 GiB memory
	Recommended by image publisher
Security type ⓘ	Standard_DS1_v2 - 1 vcpu, 3.5 GiB memory
Image * ⓘ	Standard_D4s_v3 - 4 vcpus, 16 GiB memory
	Standard_E2s_v3 - 2 vcpus, 16 GiB memory
Azure Spot instance ⓘ	See all sizes
Size * ⓘ	Standard_D2s_v3 - 2 vcpus, 8 GiB memory ⌄

Consumption

Pay-as-you-go has been a consistent theme throughout, and that's the cloud payment model where you pay for the resources that you use during a billing cycle. If you use more compute this cycle, you pay more. If you use less in the current cycle, you pay less. It's a straight forward pricing mechanism that allows for maximum flexibility.

However, Azure also offers the ability to commit to using a set amount of cloud resources in advance and receiving discounts on those "reserved" resources. Many services, including databases, compute, and storage all provide the option to commit to a level of use and receive a discount, in some cases up to 72 percent.

When you reserve capacity, you're committing to using and paying for a certain amount of Azure resources during a given period (typically one or three years). With the back-up of pay-as-you-go, if you see a sudden surge in demand that eclipses what you've pre-reserved, you just pay for the additional resources in excess of your reservation. This model allows you to recognize significant savings on reliable, consistent workloads while also having the flexibility to rapidly increase your cloud footprint as the need arises.

Maintenance

The flexibility of the cloud makes it possible to rapidly adjust resources based on demand. Using resource groups can help keep all of your resources organized. In order to control costs, it's important to maintain your cloud environment. For example, every time you provision a VM, additional resources such as storage and networking are also provisioned. If you deprovision the VM, those additional resources may not deprovision at the same time, either intentionally or unintentionally. By keeping an eye on your resources and making sure you're not keeping around resources that are no longer needed, you can help control cloud costs.

Geography

When you provision most resources in Azure, you need to define a region where the resource deploys. Azure infrastructure is distributed globally, which enables you to deploy your services centrally or closest to your customers, or something in between. With this global deployment comes global pricing differences. The cost of power, labor, taxes, and fees vary depending on the location. Due to these variations, Azure resources can differ in costs to deploy depending on the region.

Network traffic is also impacted based on geography. For example, it's less expensive to move information within Europe than to move information from Europe to Asia or South America.

Network Traffic

Billing zones are a factor in determining the cost of some Azure services.

Bandwidth refers to data moving in and out of Azure datacenters. Some inbound data transfers (data going into Azure datacenters) are free. For outbound data transfers (data leaving Azure datacenters), data transfer pricing is based on zones.

A zone is a geographical grouping of Azure regions for billing purposes.

Subscription type

Some Azure subscription types also include usage allowances, which affect costs.

For example, an Azure free trial subscription provides access to a number of Azure products that are free for 12 months. It also includes credit to spend within your first 30 days of sign-up. You'll get access to more than 25 products that are always free (based on resource and region availability).

Azure Marketplace

Azure Marketplace lets you purchase Azure-based solutions and services from third-party vendors. This could be a server with software preinstalled and configured, or managed network firewall appliances, or connectors to third-party backup services. When you purchase products through Azure Marketplace, you may pay for not only the Azure services that you're using, but also the services or expertise of the third-party vendor. Billing structures are set by the vendor.

All solutions available in Azure Marketplace are certified and compliant with Azure policies and standards. The certification policies may vary based on the service or solution type and Azure service involved.

Compare the Pricing and Total Cost of Ownership calculators

The pricing calculator and the total cost of ownership (TCO) calculator are two calculators that help you understand potential Azure expenses. Both calculators are accessible from the internet, and both calculators allow you to build out a configuration. However, the two calculators have very different purposes.

Pricing calculator

The pricing calculator is designed to give you an estimated cost for provisioning resources in Azure. You can get an estimate for individual resources, build out a solution, or use an example scenario to see an estimate of the Azure spend. The pricing calculator's focus is on the cost of provisioned resources in Azure.

With the pricing calculator, you can estimate the cost of any provisioned resources, including compute, storage, and associated network costs. You can even account for different storage options like storage type, access tier, and redundancy.

TCO calculator

The TCO calculator is designed to help you compare the costs for running an on-premises infrastructure compared to an Azure Cloud infrastructure. With the TCO calculator, you enter your current infrastructure configuration, including servers, databases, storage, and outbound network traffic. The TCO calculator then compares the anticipated costs for your current environment with an Azure environment supporting the same infrastructure requirements.

With the TCO calculator, you enter your configuration, add in assumptions like power and IT labor costs, and are presented with an estimation of the cost difference to run the same environment in your current datacenter or in Azure.

Purpose Of Azure Blueprints

What happens when your cloud starts to grow beyond just one subscription or environment? How can you scale the configuration of features? How can you enforce settings and policies in new subscriptions?

Azure Blueprints lets you standardize cloud subscription or environment deployments. Instead of having to configure features like Azure Policy for each new subscription, with Azure Blueprints you can define repeatable settings and policies that are applied as new subscriptions are created. Need a new test/dev environment? Azure Blueprints lets you deploy a new Test/Dev environment with security and compliance settings already configured. In this way, development teams can rapidly build and deploy new environments with the knowledge that they're building within organizational requirements.

What are artifacts?

Each component in the blueprint definition is known as an artifact.

It is possible for artifacts to have no additional parameters (configurations). An example is the Deploy threat detection on SQL servers policy, which requires no additional configuration.

Artifacts can also contain one or more parameters that you can configure. The following screenshot shows the Allowed locations policy. This policy includes a parameter that specifies the allowed locations.

Allowed locations

This policy enables you to restrict the locations your organization can specify when deploying resources. Use to enforce your geo-compliance requirements. Excludes resource groups, Microsoft.AzureActiveDirectory/b2cDirectories, and resources that use the 'global' region.

ⓘ You can choose to fill these parameters in now or when assigning the blueprint.

Allowed locations

0 selected   ⌄

☑ This value should be specified when the blueprint is assigned

You can specify a parameter's value when you create the blueprint definition or when you assign the blueprint definition to a scope. In this way, you can maintain one standard blueprint but have the flexibility to specify the relevant configuration parameters at each scope where the definition is assigned.

Azure Blueprints deploy a new environment based on all of the requirements, settings, and configurations of the associated artifacts. Artifacts can include things such as:

• Role assignments
• Policy assignments
• Azure Resource Manager templates
• Resource groups

How do Azure Blueprints help monitor deployments?

Azure Blueprints are version-able, allowing you to create an initial configuration and then make updates later on and assign a new version to the update. With versioning, you can make small updates and keep track of which deployments used which configuration set.

With Azure Blueprints, the relationship between the blueprint definition (what should be deployed) and the blueprint assignment (what was deployed) is preserved. In other words, Azure creates a record that associates a resource with the blueprint that defines it. This connection helps you track and audit your deployments.

The Purpose Of Azure Policy

How do you ensure that your resources stay compliant? Can you be alerted if a resource's configuration has changed?

Azure Policy is a service in Azure that enables you to create, assign, and manage policies that control or audit your resources. These policies enforce different rules across your resource configurations so that those configurations stay compliant with corporate standards.

How does Azure Policy define policies?

Azure Policy enables you to define both individual policies and groups of related policies, known as initiatives. Azure Policy evaluates your resources and highlights resources that aren't compliant with the policies you've created. Azure Policy can also prevent noncompliant resources from being created.

Azure Policies can be set at each level, enabling you to set policies on a specific resource, resource group, subscription, and so on. Additionally, Azure Policies are inherited, so if you set a policy at a high level, it will automatically be applied to all of the groupings that fall within the parent. For example, if you set an Azure Policy on a resource group, all resources created within that resource group will automatically receive the same policy.

Azure Policy comes with built-in policy and initiative definitions for Storage, Networking, Compute, Security Center, and Monitoring. For example, if you define a policy that allows only a certain size for the virtual machines (VMs) to be used in your environment, that policy is invoked when you create a new VM and whenever you resize existing VMs. Azure Policy also evaluates and monitors all current VMs in your environment, including VMs that were created before the policy was created.

In some cases, Azure Policy can automatically remediate noncompliant resources and configurations to ensure the integrity of the state of the resources. For example, if all resources in a certain resource group should be tagged with AppName tag and a value of "SpecialOrders," Azure Policy will automatically apply that tag if it is missing. However, you still retain full control of your environment. If you have a specific resource that you don't want Azure Policy to automatically fix, you can flag that resource as an exception – and the policy won't automatically fix that resource.

Azure Policy also integrates with Azure DevOps by applying any continuous integration and delivery pipeline policies that pertain to the pre-deployment and post-deployment phases of your applications.

What are Azure Policy initiatives?

An Azure Policy initiative is a way of grouping related policies together. The initiative definition contains all of the policy definitions to help track your compliance state for a larger goal.

For example, Azure Policy includes an initiative named Enable Monitoring in Azure Security Center. Its goal is to monitor all available security recommendations for all Azure resource types in Azure Security Center.

Under this initiative, the following policy definitions are included:

- **Monitor unencrypted SQL Database in Security Center** This policy monitors for unencrypted SQL databases and servers.
- **Monitor OS vulnerabilities in Security Center** This policy monitors servers that don't satisfy the configured OS vulnerability baseline.
- **Monitor missing Endpoint Protection in Security Center** This policy monitors for servers that don't have an installed endpoint protection agent.

In fact, the Enable Monitoring in Azure Security Center initiative contains over 100 separate policy definitions.

The Purpose Of Resource Locks

A resource lock prevents resources from being accidentally deleted or changed.

Even with Azure role-based access control (Azure RBAC) policies in place, there's still a risk that people with the right level of access could delete critical cloud resources. Resource locks prevent resources from being deleted or updated, depending on the type of lock. Resource locks can be applied to individual resources, resource groups, or even an entire subscription. Resource locks are inherited, meaning that if you place a resource lock on a resource group, all of the resources within the resource group will also have the resource lock applied.

Types of Resource Locks

There are two types of resource locks, one that prevents users from deleting and one that prevents users from changing or deleting a resource.

- Delete means authorized users can still read and modify a resource, but they can't delete the resource.
- ReadOnly means authorized users can read a resource, but they can't delete or update the resource. Applying this lock is similar to restricting all authorized users to the permissions granted by the Reader role.

How do I manage resource locks?

You can manage resource locks from the Azure portal, PowerShell, the Azure CLI, or from an Azure Resource Manager template.

To view, add, or delete locks in the Azure portal, go to the Settings section of any resource's Settings pane in the Azure portal.

How do I delete or change a locked resource?

Although locking helps prevent accidental changes, you can still make changes by following a two-step process.

To modify a locked resource, you must first remove the lock. After you remove the lock, you can apply any action you have permissions to perform. Resource locks apply regardless of RBAC permissions. Even if you're an owner of the resource, you must still remove the lock before you can perform the blocked activity.

GLOSSARY

- Cloud computing: The delivery of computing services, including servers, storage, databases, networking, software, analytics, and intelligence, over the Internet.
- Infrastructure as a service (IaaS): A cloud computing service model that provides virtualized computing

resources, such as servers, storage, and networking, over the Internet.

- Platform as a service (PaaS): A cloud computing service model that provides a platform for developing, deploying, and managing applications, without the need to manage the underlying infrastructure.
- Software as a service (SaaS): A cloud computing service model that provides access to software applications over the Internet, typically on a subscription basis.
- Virtual machine (VM): A software emulation of a physical computer that can run its own operating system and applications.
- Azure portal: A web-based console for managing Azure resources and services.
- Resource group: A logical container for Azure resources that share the same lifecycle, permissions, and policies.
- Availability zone: A physically separate datacenter within an Azure region that provides redundancy and high availability for Azure services.
- Load balancer: A network device that distributes incoming traffic across multiple backend servers to improve performance, scalability, and availability.
- Azure Active Directory (Azure AD): A cloud-based identity and access management service that provides authentication and authorization services

for applications and resources across Azure and other Microsoft services.

- Azure Security Center: A unified security management solution that provides threat protection for workloads running in Azure, as well as on-premises and in other clouds.
- Azure Key Vault: A cloud-based service that allows you to securely store and manage cryptographic keys, secrets, and certificates.

In conclusion, the Azure Fundamentals (AZ-900) certification exam is designed to test your basic knowledge of cloud computing and Azure services. It covers topics such as cloud concepts, Azure services, security and compliance, and pricing and support.

To prepare for the exam, you can use various resources such as Microsoft's official study guide, online courses, and practice exams. It's important to have a good understanding of the topics and concepts covered on the exam to ensure that you are adequately prepared.

By passing the AZ-900 exam, you can demonstrate your foundational knowledge of Azure and cloud computing, which can be useful for pursuing further Azure certifications or for working in cloud-related roles.

www.ingramcontent.com/pod-product-compliance
Lightning Source LLC
Chambersburg PA
CBHW052142070326
40690CB00047B/1541